To Paul Hopper
a worthy co-panelist

[signature]

Jan. 1762

THE LIMITS OF FREEDOM

The Limits of Freedom

DAVID FELLMAN

Rutgers University Press
New Brunswick, New Jersey   1959

for Laura and Michael

The 1959 Brown and Haley Lectures are the seventh of a series that has been given annually at the College of Puget Sound, Tacoma, Washington, by a scholar distinguished for his work in Social Studies or the Humanities. The purpose of these lectures is to present original analyses of some intellectual problems confronting the present age.

Foreword

The American people, in their political theory and public law, have, for over two centuries, been committed to the primacy of civil liberties in the constellation of human interests. There can be no inappropriate time for the exposition and defense of the basic freedoms without which life for us would not be worth living. And particularly a period of troubles, when the pressure to cut corners is very great, is no time to downgrade these freedoms as a concession to the necessities of emergency and world crisis. It is precisely in an age of crisis that it is most important to stand our ground and defend what is right.

Nevertheless, it is equally true that none of these rights

is absolute, since all rights exist in a state of society, not anarchy, and necessarily jostle each other. Where rights conflict with each other, choices must be made. And at some point the rights of the individual collide with the rights of others or with those of society. It is therefore never inappropriate to call attention to the limits of freedom, for the only freedom we can possibly live with is one in which an equilibrium is found between competing interests, all of which carry great validity taken singly.

In these lectures I have sought to spell out some of the inescapable limits of freedom in several of the most cherished areas of civil liberties: freedom of religion, the freedom to communicate ideas, and particularly the right to talk politics. While I believe that freedom is the rule, and that restraint upon freedom is at best the exception, to be justified by strongly persuasive considerations, nevertheless it is the part of wisdom to recognize both the inevitability and the desirability of the exceptions. I seek in these lectures to find the balance between freedom and license insofar as that balance has been worked out in American constitutional law.

These discourses were originally given in May, 1959, at the College of Puget Sound, where I had the distinguished honor of giving the Brown and Haley lectures. My week in Tacoma was a thoroughly enjoyable and stimulating one, and I take this opportunity to express my gratitude to the faculty and the students of the College for their warm hospitality and friendly and interested attention. In particular I desire to thank President R. Franklin Thompson, Dr. John D. Regester, Dean of the Faculty, Professor Lyle S. Shelmidine of the Department of History, and Mr. and Mrs. Fred T. Haley for the many acts of kindness and consideration which were extended to me and my wife during a very memorable week. I cannot refrain from expressing the hope that the Brown and Haley lectureship will have a long and distinguished career in American scholarship. As a Brown and Haley alumnus, I shall always try to give it a full measure of devotion.

David Fellman

June 1959
Madison, Wisconsin

THE LIMITS OF FREEDOM

1 *Religious Freedom in America—More or Less*

1

No commitment of the American people is more widely and deeply held, and more fully articulated, than the principle of religious freedom, and its corollary, the separation of church and state. A broad-gauged guaranty of religious freedom is spelled out in the First Amendment of the federal Constitution and in the constitution of every state. The underlying rationale of religious freedom has been elaborated by great Americans in all periods of our history, by Roger Williams and William Penn in colonial times, by Thomas Jefferson and James Madison in the days of the formation of the present Union, by members of Congress, Presidents, and Supreme Court Justices, by great educators like Horace Mann, and by philosophers and theologians of many schools of thought.[1]

Foreign observers of the American scene have always been impressed with this aspect of our culture and government. Writing in 1893, Lord Bryce remarked, in what is still one of the best books ever written about the American governmental system: "Of all the differences between the Old World and the New this is perhaps the most salient. Half the wars of Europe, half the internal troubles that have vexed European States, from the Monophysite controversies in the Roman Empire of the fifth century down to the *Kulturkampf* in the German Empire of the nineteenth, have arisen from theological differences or from the rival claims of Church and State. This whole vast chapter of debate and strife has remained virtually unopened in the United States. There is no Established Church. All religious bodies are absolutely equal before the law, and unrecognized by the law, except as voluntary associations of private citizens."[2]

Long before Bryce's time, another distinguished foreign observer toured this country in the early 1830's, Alexis de Tocqueville. He was struck by the fact, as was Bryce, that although there is a separation of church and state in America, religion was in a very healthy condition, possessing influence rather than power. Himself a Catholic, he recorded that he spoke to several priests about the astonishing strength of religion in the United States. "I found," he wrote, "that they differed upon matters of detail alone, and that they all attributed the peaceful dominion of religion in their country mainly to the separation of church and state. I do not hesitate to affirm that during my stay in America I did not meet a single individual, of the clergy or the laity, who was not of the same opinion on this point." [3] Similarly, Lord Bryce noted that "there seem to be no two opinions on this subject in the United States. Even the Protestant Episcopal clergy, who are in many ways disposed to admire and feel with their brethren in England; even the Roman Catholic bishops, whose creed justifies the enforcement of the true faith by the secular arm, assure the European visitor that if State establishment were offered them they would decline it, preferring the freedom they enjoy to any advantages the State could confer." [4]

Nevertheless, though the principles of freedom of religion and separation of church and state are deeply rooted, neither can, in a workaday world, be carried out literally and absolutely. In fact, many of the very constitutional provisions which state these principles indicate the necessity of recognizing certain limitations. For example, the New York Constitution guarantees "the free exercise and enjoyment of religious profession and worship, without discrimination or preference, . . . to all mankind"; but it goes on to say that "the liberty of conscience hereby secured shall not be so construed as to excuse acts of licentiousness, or justify practices inconsistent with the peace or safety of this State." [5] All American courts agree that some such general proposition as this is wholly valid, but the definition of the requirements of the peace and safety of the state is fraught with great difficulties. It has never been a simple task to draw the proper boundary line between freedom and license in any field of human activity.

2

How very difficult it is to locate this line is reflected, to cite a widely known example, in the state's dealings with extremist, faith-healing cults. Americans have always had a penchant for utopian, perfectionist, emotional, fundamentalist, and millennial cults which purport to have sure remedies for disease and other forms of human misery. One specialist historian recently estimated that the cult world is populated by about 5,000,000 "ardent Americans." [6] In fact, over a century ago De Tocqueville, who noted the manifestations of fanatical spiritualism in this country, observed how "from time to time strange sects arise which endeavor to strike out extraordinary paths to eternal happiness." And he concluded with the laconic observation that "religious insanity is very common in the United States." [7]

The cult world is a troubled and unsettled area of American life in which claims asserted in the name of some sort of religion collide with the legitimate concern of the state to protect people against being bilked by dishonest operators. The great difficulties involved here were illustrated by a much-discussed case which reached the Supreme Court in 1944.[8] It involved a federal mail fraud prosecution of the founders and leaders of a religious cult known as the "I Am." According to the testimony, the cult began when Guy Ballard, its principal figure, wrote a book at Mount Shasta, California, entitled *Unveiled Mysteries.* Actually, he claimed that he did not write the book himself, but merely wrote down what was dictated to him by St. Germain. (St. Germain, or Germanus, the Bishop of Auxerre, had gone to his everlasting reward in 448.) Ballard taught that he, as well as his wife Edna and his son Donald, had been selected by St. Germain as divine messengers because of their high spiritual attainments and righteous conduct. They said they had been accorded a supernatural state of self-immortality of body as a consequence of supernatural visitation. They taught that in an intermediate sphere between God and man exist many Ascended Masters or Divine Beings, who are especially devoted to the assistance of mankind in the attainment of high moral standards, harmony and eventual salvation. They said that only because of their teachings, influence, and movement has the United States been saved from destruction, and that on one occasion they saved San Francisco from disaster. They said that a cataclysm, or end of the world, was approaching. They taught that those who follow the doctrines of "I Am" will not die, but will "ascend," not in their physical, tangible bodies, but in their etheric bodies, and associate with the divine entities and Ascended Masters. Thereafter they will be able to return to earth at will, and "reascend" if they so desire. There was evidence to show that Mrs. Ballard had represented that the Ballards had shaken hands with Jesus as well as with St. Germain. There was also a great deal of talk about precipitation; believers would be able to precipitate gold, jewels, and other material needs from the air. Indeed, the "I Am" teachings were thickly studded with such words and phrases as "invisible plane," "Great Law," "I Am Presence," "The Magic Presence," "Goddess of Light," "Divine Director," "Violet Consuming Flame," and the like.

At the trial a great deal of testimony was concerned

with the Ballards' claim to the possession of supernatural healing powers. There was much testimony to the fact that the Ballards had indicated that by reason of their being divine messengers they had great healing powers, and that "I Am" followers could acquire such powers and achieve perfect bodies by giving implicit obedience to the teachings and precepts of the movement. At the trial Mrs. Ballard testified that her husband had healed 20,000 people in a period of eight years.[9] There was considerable testimony to the effect that the Ballards had represented that they could cure incurable diseases, including cancer, old age, poverty, misery, and even death itself. They said they could heal dismembered legs and blindness.

A great many people testified for the defense at the trial, including an M.D., a dentist, a registered nurse, a Ph.D. in education, a Ph.D. in science, an attorney, a stockbroker, a chemical engineer, a few civil servants, and several businessmen, including a banker. They all said that they derived solace and greater peace of mind from the "I Am" teachings. One witness, the mother of seven children, testified that she had been "healed from paralysis, diabetes, an acute heart condition, very serious nervous disorders," pneumonia, neuritis, arthritis, inflammatory rheumatism, and malaria fever. At this point the prosecutor asked her, "Did you ever hear of the word 'hypochondria'?" To which the witness replied,

"I am not a walking dictionary." [10] The wife of a blind United States Senator testified that on one occasion she asked Mrs. Ballard about the Senator's affliction, to which this reply was made: "She told me to visualize a ray of light from His Mighty I Am Presence down through the top of his head and turning at right angles and going to his eyes and that this would cure his blindness along with his attendance at classes and reading the books and following out the doctrines in the books." [11] The Senator began to read the books in October, 1935, and on December 21, 1935, this unfortunate man was struck by an automobile and killed. His widow also testified that "Mrs. Ballard said that through precipitation it was quite possible to keep spots off of clothing; that she always wore light gowns and called on the Mighty I Am to keep the spots off." [12]

Some of Edna Ballard's views on health questions were most illuminating. She testified at the trial: "We do not use tobacco nor liquor, alcoholic beverages, because they dry up secretions in the brain and that prevents the clear, intelligent direction from each one's source of life of the mighty I Am presence from being clear in the intellect and allowing real intelligence and discrimination and the constructive impulses to hold control of the energy of the body." She also said: "We do not use animal food. Not because of any sentiment but because all animals know anywhere from 24 to 48 hours before they are going to be killed they are to be killed. They feel it. That charges the flesh, their meat— the flesh, I would rather put it that way—with a rate of vibration of fear. The human being that puts that sub- stance into the body has to handle that rate of vibration, and that is what has created a great deal of cancer in the last 25 years in the United States of America, because wherever the meat eating is increased, you always have an increase of cancer, increase of insanity, and increase of immorality." [13]

The I Am movement was established as a corporation known as the Saint Germain Foundation. As a subsidi- ary, the Ballards created another corporation known as the Saint Germain Press, which published and sold books, charts, pamphlets, magazines, pictures, and pho- nograph records made of some blue substance. The blue was supposed to have some special vitalizing quality. In addition to *Unveiled Mysteries,* Ballard published *The Magic Presence, The I Am Discourses, The Ascended Masters Discourses, The I Am Adorations and Affirma- tions, The I Am Decrees* (in loose-leaf), and *The As- cended Master Light.* These books were all dictated by St. Germain to Guy Ballard, with Edna correcting the spelling and punctuation. In addition, the Ballards maintained branch offices, meeting rooms, and reading

rooms in various cities, and conducted many radio programs. They were energetic and enterprising, ingenious
and ingenuous.

The principal sources of income were from the re-
ceipt of Love Gifts and the sale of books, charts, pictures, records, et cetera. While the Ballards insisted that
they never solicited money directly, it is clear that they
received large sums of money. In addition, their profit
margin on the various types of printed matter was quite
substantial. In fact, the hundreds of letters put into the
trial record were full of references to and haggling over
money matters. But, of course, as the Ballard attorneys
asserted in their Supreme Court brief, "Money is con-
stantly requested of the members in every religious denomination." [14]

The government's theory in bringing this prosecution
was that the Ballards had used the mails for fraudulent
purposes. The chief prosecutor summed up his point of
view in his closing argument when he declared that
"crime is no less odious because it is shellacked with a
little bit of religion." [15] But the great issue in the case,
from the very start, was concerned with the question of
what was proper for the jury to decide. What aspect of
this pattern of behavior should be submitted to the
jury? What questions arising from religious experience
may be tried in a civil court, and which are outside the
scope of the secular laws of the state? For example,

should the jury be asked to decide whether it believed that Guy Ballard had shaken hands with St. Germain, or whether it believed that Ballard had in fact cured the incurable?

Early in the trial the judge adopted a theory which subsequently controlled the admission of evidence, and which he presented to the jury in his final instructions. His theory was that the soundness, or truth, or even the plausibility, of the "I Am" doctrines was not for the jury to rule on. The only proper question for the jury to decide, the judge held, was whether the defendants honestly and in good faith believed the things they preached. Thus, in his final instructions he told the jury that the lawfulness of the calling of a mental or religious healer was not in question. Healing by prayer, he said, was as lawful as healing by drugs. Whereas it is not for the jury to pass on the truth or falsity of religious beliefs and doctrines, the judge said that "even though a person or persons are advocating a religious activity, . . . they must do so in good faith and without making any substantial misrepresentations with the intent to deceive."

On these instructions the case went to the jury. Guy Ballard was out of the picture by this time, having died in Los Angeles on December 29, 1939, after an operation. Edna Ballard was found guilty on seven counts, sentenced to a year's imprisonment on each, the sentences to run concurrently, and fined $8,000. Donald was given a sentence of thirty days in jail on three counts, and fined $400. The prison sentences were suspended, however, and the Ballards were placed on probation for one year.

The Ballards appealed to the Court of Appeals for the Ninth Circuit, which reversed the conviction on the ground that the basic theory of the trial judge, which distinguished between the verity and sincerity of the defendants' beliefs, was erroneous.[16] On further appeal, the Supreme Court reversed the Court of Appeals, holding that the trial judge's instructions were consistent with the requirements of American constitutional law. Counsel for the Ballards argued in vain that a trial of either the veracity of religious beliefs or the bad faith in such beliefs was "wholly impractical in a country with such a divergency of beliefs as ours." [17] They insisted that it was just as difficult to prove good faith belief to people of other religions as it would be to establish its truth. Since jurors cannot reconcile their beliefs with those of the Ballards, counsel argued, they will almost invariably make a finding of bad faith.[18]

Speaking for the Court, Justice Douglas declared that the trial judge had ruled properly when he withheld from the jury all questions concerning the truth or falsity of the religious beliefs and doctrines of the Ballards, since this is required by the First Amendment guaranty of religious freedom. In a society of free men, said Justice Douglas, freedom of religious thought is basic. "It embraces the right to maintain theories of life and of death and of the hereafter which are rank heresy to followers of the orthodox faiths. Heresy trials are foreign to our Constitution. Men may believe what they cannot prove. They may not be put to the proof of their religious doctrines or beliefs. Religious experiences which are as real as life to some may be incomprehensible to others. Yet the fact that they may be beyond the ken of mortals does not mean that they can be made suspect before the law." [19] He went on to say: "Many take their gospel from the New Testament. But it would hardly be supposed that they could be tried before a jury charged with the duty of determining whether those teachings contained false representations. The miracles of the New Testament, the Divinity of Christ, life after death, the power of prayer, are deep in the religious convictions of many. If one could be sent to jail because a jury in a hostile environment found those teachings false, little indeed would be left of religious freedom." [20]

The authors of the Constitution, Justice Douglas asserted, were aware of this country's religious diversity, and therefore fashioned a charter permitting "the widest possible toleration of conflicting views. Man's relation to his God was made no concern of the state. He was granted the right to worship as he pleased and to

answer to no man for the verity of his religious views." [21]
Although the religious views of the Ballards might seem
incredible, and even preposterous, to most people, Justice Douglas noted that if the truth or falsity of these
views is subject to trial before a jury, then the same can
be done with the beliefs of any religious sect. "When the
triers of fact undertake that task," he wrote, "they enter
a forbidden domain. The First Amendment does not
select any one group or any one type of religion for preferred treatment. It puts them all in that position." [22]

A bare majority of the Court voted to remand the case
to the Court of Appeals for the disposition of other issues. Chief Justice Stone spoke for the three members
of the Court who thought that the convictions should
stand because they felt there was ample evidence to support the jury's finding that the defendants had not believed in the truth of their own statements. The Chief
Justice declared that he was "not prepared to say that
the constitutional guaranty of freedom of religion af-
fords immunity from criminal prosecution for the
fraudulent procurement of money by false statements
as to one's religious experiences, more than it renders
polygamy or libel immune from criminal prosecution.
. . . I cannot say that freedom of thought and worship
includes freedom to procure money by making knowingly false statements about one's religious experiences." [23]

Justice Jackson dissented alone on the merits, taking the position that this trial should never have occurred. Although he could see nothing in the Ballards' teaching "but humbug, untainted by any trace of truth," he strongly felt that no religious beliefs are constitutionally indictable. He felt that it was impossible to "separate an issue as to what is believed from considerations as to what is believable." [24] The normal test of whether one believes something to be false is whether it is proved to be false. Furthermore, Justice Jackson argued that it is psychologically impossible for juries to separate fancied from real religious experiences; and such experiences, he insisted, cannot be verified in the minds of people who are without religious insight. All religions, he noted, "make enormous assumptions, generally on the basis of revelations authenticated by some sign or miraacle." [25]

Justice Jackson went on to say: "There appear to be persons—let us hope not many—who find refreshment and courage in the teachings of the 'I Am' cult. If the members of the sect get comfort from the celestial guidance of their 'Saint Germain,' however doubtful it seems to me, it is hard to say that they do not get what they pay for. Scores of sects flourish in this country by teaching what to me are queer notions. It is plain that there is wide variety in American religious taste. The Ballards are not alone in catering to it with a pretty dubious product." [26] He added that the chief wrong was not financial, but rather on the spiritual plane; when men who hunger for "truth and beauty and moral support" are deluded, cynicism and confusion follow. The wrong "is in the mental and spiritual poison they get," but this is precisely what the Constitution puts beyond the reach of the prosecutor; for the price we pay for freedom of religion is "that we must put with, and even pay for, a good deal of rubbish." [27] Thus, Justice Jackson concluded that he would dismiss the indictment, "and have done with this business of judicially examining other people's faiths."

Of the positions taken by the Justices in the Ballard case, Justice Jackson's would seem to be the most consistent with the spirit of the American constitutional guaranty of religious freedom. The view that the jury should be allowed to rule on the truth or falsity of religious doctrines is clearly contrary to the guaranty, and all the Justices agreed on this point. But even the compromise solution of the Court majority, which rules out any consideration of verity of religious experience, but requires honest belief in their actuality, presents grave difficulties. Whereas the distinction between fact and belief might stand up in commercial matters, it is much less tenable in the case of religious experiences. It is difficult to believe that very many jurors will conclude that the accused honestly believed something which they, the jurors, consider unbelievable. Furthermore, it is quite possible that a great many contemporary clergymen in the most respectable faiths who accept offerings of money do not privately believe that everything they profess is true. If this is the measure of criminal fraud, the floodgates of criminal prosecution may well be opened wider than anyone would really want them to be.

3

Though Justice Jackson's position is preferable to that taken by Justice Douglas, it cannot be denied that the majority point of view is basically friendly to religious freedom. Indeed, American courts, state and federal, have on the whole proceeded on the assumption that freedom of religion is essential, and that restraints upon that freedom are wholly exceptionable and not sustainable except upon a very strong showing of vital public interest.

The various freedoms that are guaranteed by American constitutional law do not really stand upon a parity of importance. In any system of values, I suppose that it is quite inevitable that some should be more highly regarded than others. In the American constellation of rights, none stands in a more preferred position than the claim to religious freedom. For the claim is deeply rooted in American historical experience, as well as in our law and philosophy.

As early as April 21, 1649, the legislature of the colony of Maryland adopted a statute providing for religious freedom, at least for all varieties of Christians, and citing three very persuasive reasons for such freedom. It was noted that "the inforceing of the conscience in matters of Religion hath frequently fallen out to be of dangerous Consequence in those commonwealthes where it hath been practised," that freedom of religion was conducive "for the more quiett and peaceable governemt" of the province, and was "the better to pserve mutuall Love and amity amongst the Inhabitants thereof." [28] At the same time the statute sought to promote peaceful relations among the people by forbidding them to call each other religious names. The statute made it a criminal offense that any person should "in a reproachful manner or Way declare call or denominate any pson or psons whatsoever inhabiting residing traffiqueing trading or comerceing within this Province . . . an heritick, Scismatick, Idolator, puritan, Independant, Prespiterian, popish prest, Jesuite, Jesuited papist, Lutheran, Calvenist, Anabaptist, Brownist, Antinomian, Barrowist, Roundhead, Se'patist, or any other name or terme in a reproachful manner relating to matter of Religion. . . ." [29]

Certainly the case for religious freedom has been stated more elegantly in later documents, as in the preamble of Thomas Jefferson's Act for Establishing Religious Freedom of 1779, or in James Madison's celebrated Memorial and Remonstrance on the Religious Rights of Man of 1784; [30] but it is clear, as Justice Black once observed, that any manifestation of governmental hostility to religion "would be at war with our national tradition." [31]

Furthermore, American constitutional tradition is committed to the proposition that the separation of church and state is essential to the enjoyment of religious freedom. They are two sides of the same coin. The First Amendment of the federal Constitution both guarantees the free exercise of religion and prohibits the establishment of any religion; and this is the pattern of state constitutional provisions. Jefferson, in the Virginia Act for Establishing Religious Freedom, declared it to be both "sinful and tyrannical" to compel a man to pay for the propagation of opinions which he disbelieves.[32] In fact, he argued that it was wholly improper for the government even to force a man to support a teacher of his own religious persuasion, since it denied him the liberty of making a choice among pastors and weakened the minister's incentive to earn approval through his own efforts.

Clearly, the separation of church and state is essential

in a country which has some 250 different religious denominations. But the multiplicity of sects is by no means the only reason for separation. Such theologians as Roger Williams, Jonathan Edwards, and George Whitefield took the position that the business of the state is simply different in kind from that of religion. Madison maintained, in his Memorial and Remonstrance, that matters of conscience are all voluntary in character, maintainable "only by reason and conviction," and therefore outside the jurisdiction of government. And what, he asked, have been the fruits of establishment? "More or less, in all places, pride and indolence in the clergy; ignorance and servility in the laity; in both, superstition, bigotry, and persecution." Deist-humanist groups also supported separation in the formative days of our nation on the basis of the assumptions of the Enlightenment. As to religion, said Thomas Paine in *Common Sense,* "I hold it to be the indispensable duty of all governments, to protect all conscientious professors thereof, and I know of no other business which government hath to do therewith." [33]

The Supreme Court of Ohio summed up this important point of view many years ago when it said: "*Legal* Christianity is a solecism, a contradiction of terms. When Christianity asks the aid of government beyond mere *impartial protection,* it denies itself. Its laws are divine, and not human. Its essential interests lie beyond the reach and range of human governments. United with government, religion never rises above the merest superstition; united with religion, government never rises above the merest despotism; and all history shows us that the more widely and completely they are separated, the better it is for both." [34]

Our commitment to separation of church and state is reflected in the fact that direct financial aid to religious institutions is illegal under the law of every state of the union. It is also worth noting that Congress has never granted direct financial aid to churches and church schools, not even non-preferential aid. Nevertheless, the available evidence certainly does not indicate that the policy of separation has hurt religion at all. It is estimated that in 1790 only about 10 per cent of the people affiliated with religious bodies. Today, after more than a century of separation, the figure is around 60 per cent.[35] Separation is good for religion, since it leaves religion free to perform its lofty spiritual functions without being chained to a worldly establishment. It is good for the state, since the latter does not have to assume the impossible task of passing judgment on religious truth and of taking sides in religious conflict. It is good for the individual, since he is left free to make his own decisions without governmental compulsion in an atmosphere of tolerance and liberty. The Federal Council of Churches declared in 1944: "The separation of church

and state has been our great bulwark of religious freedom in America. It has insured a policy of equal treatment of all religious bodies by the national government.
It has afforded to every church an equal opportunity to
develop its inherent possibilities. It has thereby provided a spiritual climate favorable to goodwill and co-
operation among Protestants, Roman Catholics and
Jews." [36]

4

Nevertheless, the churches do not and cannot function
in a social and political vacuum. At many points their
rights and obligations are defined by or are dependent
upon the law of the state. Where they own property, for
example, they are inextricably connected with government, since whatever else property rights may be, they
are indisputably legal rights. Thus, when two factions
of the same congregation dispute the right to occupy a
church building, the civil courts have jurisdiction to
determine the proper occupant. To be sure, in the case
of hierarchical churches, American courts will do no
more than determine the position of the appropriate
church authorities, if it is at all possible to do so.[37] But

in any event, the state cannot sit by idly and permit religious factions to settle their property disputes by violence. It intervenes to keep the peace, while at the same time it tries to avoid being involved in controversies over religious dogmas and beliefs.

The most familiar illustrations of the limits of religious freedom are found in situations where the peace, safety, and good order of the community impose them. It is clear that however large the area of religious freedom may be, and however reluctant the courts may be to set limits to that freedom, there are countervailing interests which are regarded as so vital to society that they serve as justification for some limitations. These interests include the protection of public morals and public health, the care of children, national defense, general welfare, and public order.

The classic example of a moral problem is that of polygamy sanctioned by religious principles. In sustaining an act of Congress which abolished polygamy in the territories, the Supreme Court declared in 1878, in a case involving Brigham Young's private secretary, George Reynolds, that although the First Amendment deprived Congress "of all legislative power over mere opinion," Congress "was left free to reach actions which were in violation of social duties or subversive of good order." [38] The Court pointed out that the practice of polygamy has always been odious to the people of Western civilization, that it was always illegal under the common law, and that it has always been a crime in every state. Thus it said in a later case that to call the advocacy of polygamy "a tenet of religion is to offend the common sense of mankind." [39] Justice Field also said, in the opinion of this case, that "crime is not the less odious because sanctioned by what any particular sect may designate as religion." Perhaps the second observation is contradictory with the first; for there can be no doubt of the fact that at one time a religious group did believe that polygamy was a tenet of religion. The point is, of course, that the appendage of a religious tag does not and cannot conclude the matter. It is also worth noting that on the question of the prohibition of polygamy by law, the Court made no effort to discover the "intent" of the men who wrote and adopted the First Amendment, since on this subject, as on so many other contemporary problems, the Founding Fathers had no intent one way or the other. The Court must ultimately draw the line between permissible and non-permissible conduct, in the light of public policy considerations comprehended in the context of contemporary conditions and moral sensibilities.

Where important interests of children are concerned, American courts often conclude that religious considerations must yield. Thus the Supreme Court held, in an important case decided in 1944, *Prince* v. *Massachu-*

setts,[40] that the requirements of the state's child labor laws take precedence over a religious practice, the sale of religious pamphlets on the streets of Boston by a young Jehovah's Witness girl. The Jehovah's Witness sect, which seems to have among its enthusiasms a passion for litigation, has won many cases in the Supreme Court—44 out of 55 since 1938 [41]—but it was noted that "neither rights of religion nor rights of parenthood are beyond limitation." [42] The state has especially broad responsibilities in connection with the welfare of children, and a measure of its concern is reflected in child labor laws. Here both parental authority and religious scruple must yield to the state's police power purpose of protecting young children from psychological or physical injury.

Whereas grown people may take the risks involved in relying upon faith healing, American law is strongly inclined to the view that the state has the right and indeed the duty to interfere where the health of minor children is concerned. "Parents," Justice Rutledge once wrote, "may be free to become martyrs themselves. But it does not follow they are free, in identical circumstances, to make martyrs of their children before they have reached the age of full and legal discretion when they can make that choice for themselves." [43] Formerly, at the common law, a parent was not criminally liable if neglect of the child's health was due to religious conviction, but this was changed in England by the enactment of a series of statutes dating from 1868, and by decisions of English courts.[44] Since the turn of the century the criminal liability of parents has been recognized by American courts.[45] In fact, more recently American state courts have taken the position that where parents refuse to take obvious and clearly efficacious medical steps, without which an infant child's life is in danger, the state may step in as *parens patriae* to take custody of the child in order to save its life.[46] This is done under the authority of statutes which seek to protect the child against the consequences of parental neglect.

Society's interest in protecting the public health and safety has often prevailed over religious claims. The courts have frequently sustained prosecutions under laws which control the conditions of medical practice in cases where medicine was practiced under the guise of faith healing, spiritualism, or fortunetelling in a religious context.[47] The question in these cases is not whether the defendant practiced his religion, but whether he practiced medicine.[48] The Oklahoma Court of Criminal Appeals once said, in an opinion dealing with fortunetelling in religious guise: "Fantastic philosophers and religious zealots, like other people, must conform to wholesome police regulations." [49] Accordingly, it has been held that people must submit to health laws and regulations—compulsory vaccination for smallpox, for example [50]—whatever their private or religious views may be. Compulsory vaccination of school children over religious objections has often been sustained by state appellate courts.[51] Similarly, a student attending a state university may not on grounds of religious conviction decline to take a chest X-ray examination designed to discover tuberculosis.[52] In addition, where the question has been raised, state courts have invariably upheld the fluoridation of public water against religious objections.[53] In the interests of health and safety, several southeastern states have adopted legislation, later approved by their highest courts, affecting snake-handling cults. These statutes either prohibit the handling of snakes in such a manner as to endanger public health, safety and welfare,[54] or altogether forbid the handling of snakes in connection with any religious service.[55] The North Carolina Supreme Court asserted that such legislation poses a simple question: "Which is superior, the public safety or the defendants' religious practice? The authorities are at one in holding that the safety of the public comes first." [56]

There have been numerous judicial decisions which underscore the proposition, as the Supreme Court once asserted, that "however free the exercise of religion may be, it must be subordinate to the criminal laws of the country. . . ." [57] In fact, the Michigan Supreme Court once stated, "the whole criminal law might be practically superseded if, under pretext of liberty of conscience, the commission of crime is made a religious dogma." [58] Thus, violation of the Mann Act cannot be condoned because of religious conviction. Such a defense claims too much, Justice Douglas wrote in 1946; for "if upheld, it would place beyond the law any act done under claim of religious sanction." [59] In cases involving religious activities, state courts have often held it proper to forbid the use of the streets in such a loud and noisy fashion as to disturb the normal and legitimate rights of others.[60] Similarly, the Supreme Court has ruled that cursing a public officer in a public place is not an exercise of religion in any sense of the term.[61] Utterances which tend to inflict injury or incite an immediate breach of the peace—including "the lewd and obscene, the profane, the libelous, and the insulting or 'fighting' words"—"are of such slight social value as a step to truth that any benefit that may be derived from them is clearly outweighed by the social interest in order and morality." [62] Thus a revivalist preacher in Kentucky was once convicted of an offense for using obscene, vulgar language in the pulpit, the court pointing out that "one will not be permitted to commit a breach of the peace, under the guise of preaching the gospel." [63] Furthermore, freedom of religion does not include the freedom to disturb the peace of occupants of housing developments through noisy and offensive conduct contrary to reasonable regulations.[64]

Speaking generally, churches and religionists are not immune from the operation of valid laws. Churches must obey building codes and zoning ordinances.[65] Increasingly, American courts are abandoning ancient common law rules to hold that religious eleemosynary institutions are subject to ordinary rules of negligence litigation,[66] though the general rule is still the other way.[67] It has been held that a state may bar a religious pacifist from the practice of law on the ground that he cannot take the required oath to support a constitution which makes all males subject to service in the militia in time of war.[68] The constitutional guaranty of religious freedom is no defense to a member of a religious sect charged with the offense of advising others to evade the Selective Service Act.[69] A state university may require ROTC training as a condition of enrollment, even in the face of religious scruple.[70] Compulsory school laws have often been sustained over religious objections.[71] The Supreme Court has ruled that a city may require a religious sect to secure a special license and pay a fee before staging a parade or procession upon the public streets, that is, as long as the licensing authority is not invested with arbitrary discretion and does not administer the rules in a discriminatory fashion.[72]

5

In short, then, in a complex society which has many vital and often competing interests, religious freedom cannot be taken as absolute. As Jeremy Bentham once observed, to give priority over the laws to any claim merely because it is advanced on religious grounds, would amount to "arming every fanatic against all governments." For, he asked, "in the immense variety of ideas respecting natural and Divine law, cannot some reason be found for resisting all human laws?" [73] But if this is true, it is equally true that it is wholly impossible, for about the same reasons, to have a complete and absolute separation of church and state. The disappointments of fanatical believers in religious freedom as an absolute are pretty well balanced by the disappointments of fanatical believers in an impenetrably high wall of separation between church and state. The anguish of the healing cultist who runs afoul of the laws against fraud must be set off against the dismay of the rigid separationist who objects to providing chaplains for Congress at public expense. If, as Chief Justice Vinson remarked in the Dennis case,[74] "nothing is more certain in modern society than the principle that there are no absolutes," this proposition holds for the separation as well as for the religious freedom principle.

A familiar example of the relativity of the principle of separation is found in the fact that every state of the union now grants tax exemption to church properties which are used for religious purposes.[75] The courts have sustained this tax exemption on broad grounds of public policy, taking the view that it is founded on the benefits that religious institutions confer upon society.[76] In a well-known case the Illinois Supreme Court once pointed out that it is important for the public good in a religious nation to foster moral and religious education, and that a non-discriminatory tax-exemption law violates no constitutional provision since it does not establish a religion or give any preferential treatment to any religious organization.[77] It should be added that as long as the policy of the state is to help all charitable institutions, the omission of religious institutions could be construed as a discrimination against religion.

While tax exemption is a friendly gesture designed to aid religion, it necessarily involves the state with religion, because if religious institutions are given exemption, then the state must decide what constitutes a religious institution. It would be unthinkable to extend tax exemption to any group merely for the asking. It may be noted that the same problem arises when public authorities are called upon to construe conscientious objector exemptions incorporated in selective service and naturalization laws.[78]

Dictionaries generally define religion in terms of faith in a Supreme Being. Thus Webster's unabridged *New International Dictionary* (1955) gives nine definitions, of which eight are couched in such terms. The first affirms that religion is "the service and adoration of God or a god as expressed in forms of worship, in obedience to divine commands, especially as found in accepted sacred writings or as declared by recognized teachers. . . ." One of the definitions, however, describes religion as "devotion or fidelity; scrupulous conformity; conscientiousness." Justice Field once declared that "the term 'religion' has reference to one's views of his relation to his Creator. . . ." [79] Chief Justice Hughes asserted in 1931 that "the essence of religion is belief in a relation to God. . . ." [80] William James defined religion as "the feelings, acts, and experiences of individual men in their solitude, so far as they apprehend themselves to stand in relation to whatever they may consider the divine." [81]

It is well known, however, that we have a considerable number of humanist societies which do not believe in a Supreme Being, but which occupy buildings that look like churches and hold meetings that resemble religious services, under the direction of leaders who act like pastors. Are these societies entitled to tax exemption? Of course, it all depends upon the construction of the term "religion," but the point is that this is a question which tax officials and ultimately the courts must answer, however much the making of such decisions runs counter to a simon-pure theory of separation. Thus in October, 1957, the United States Court of Appeals for the District of Columbia by unanimous vote set aside the holdings of the Tax Assessor and the Tax Court of the District to hold that the Washington Ethical Society was entitled to exemption from taxation on its buildings, within the meaning of an act of Congress exempting "religious corporations or societies." [82] The Court noted that the Ethical Society held regular Sunday services with the usual forms of worship, and had "leaders" who preached and members who were ministered to, as regards "naming, marrying and burying." The Court asserted that the term "religion" is not a rigid concept, and that definitions found in dictionaries are not free from ambiguity. In granting tax exemption, the Court ruled, Congress, like most of the states, "was giving expression to a broad legislative purpose to grant support to elements in the community regarded as good for the community." Noting that various educational, medical, charitable, and patriotic societies are also given tax exemption, the Court said: "To construe exemptions so strictly that unorthodox or minority forms of worship would be denied the exemption benefits granted to those conforming to the majority beliefs might well raise constitutional questions."

In September, 1957, a similar decision was handed down by a California Court of Appeals in a case involving the Fellowship of Humanity in Oakland.[83] The Court noted that "there are forms of belief generally and commonly accepted as religions and whose adherents, numbering in the millions, practice what is commonly accepted as religious worship, which do not include or require as essential the belief in a deity. Taoism, classic Buddhism, and Confucianism, are among these religions." The Court found that the dictionary definitions were "not conclusive," and said that a narrow definition would not be consistent with our traditions of religious tolerance. Since the Court believed that it was wholly improper for civil authorities to examine the validity or contents of religious beliefs, it held that only an objective test will suffice; and it concluded that a religion must include a belief (not necessarily involving supernatural powers), a cult, a system of moral practice based on the belief, and an organization designed for the observance of the belief's tenets. Under this test it is clearly immaterial whether the beliefs of the Society are theistic or non-theistic.

The pages of American experience bristle with illustrations of the proposition that a wall of separation so very high and solid as to preclude any contacts at all between state and church is wholly unthinkable. As early as 1815 the Supreme Court had occasion to defend a church's title to realty against the attempt of a state to appropriate, and to hold that the granting to a church of a corporate charter was not contrary to principles of religious freedom.[84] In 1899, the Court unanimously sustained a federal appropriation for the building of an isolation ward on the property of a Catholic hospital in Washington.[85] During World War I the Court said that it was so obvious as not to merit argument that the exemption of ordained ministers, theological students, and religious conscientious objectors from military service was not inconsistent with constitutional doctrine relating to state-church relationships.[86] Sunday closing laws are universally upheld in this country, not on religious grounds, but on the theory that the state has the right "to protect all persons from physical and moral debasement, which comes from uninterrupted labor." [87]

It is in the field of education that the principal church-state issues are agitated today.[88] If separation were perfect, there would be no religion in the public schools, and no state aid would go to the religious schools. Actually, the courts have sanctioned many deviations from complete separation insofar as education is concerned. Although the public school, like the government, is a civil and secular institution,[89] a great many states permit or even require Bible-reading, and more state supreme courts have ruled in favor of Bible-reading than the other way.[90] In 1948, the Supreme Court held that the separation principle, as applied to the states through the Due Process Clause of the Fourteenth Amendment, forbids the giving of sectarian instruction in public schools during school time.[91] But by 1952 it withdrew to the position that such instruction was permissible if the children left the school building, though still on school time.[92] To be sure, many critics, including three dissenting Justices, felt that from the point of view of constitutional principle the distinction between released and dismissed time was not as substantial as all that; but, as Justice Douglas said in the second case, the public service must be accommodated to the spiritual needs of a religious people. He asserted: "The First Amendment . . . does not say that in every and all respects there shall be a separation of Church and State. Rather, it studiously defines the manner, the specific ways, in which there shall be no concert or union or dependency one on the other. That is the common sense of the matter. Otherwise the state and religion would be aliens to each other—hostile, suspicious, and even unfriendly." [93] Even so, the Court believes that requiring public school pupils to salute the flag over religious objection goes too far.[94]

The state may require children to get an education in some approved fashion, whether in a public or private school or under the direction of licensed tutors, whatever may be the religious convictions of the parents.[95] But in a historic decision made in 1925 the Supreme Court made it crystal clear that the state may not constitutionally require children to attend a public school.[96] And while private schools must comply with reasonable educational standards prescribed by the state, the Court ruled that a state acted unreasonably when it forbade the teaching of a modern foreign language in a German-language Lutheran parochial school.[97]

It is contrary to law in every state to grant tax money directly to private schools.[98] Just recently, the highest courts of Vermont and Virginia ruled that it was contrary either to statute or constitutional law to pay public funds to parents to enable them to pay tuition to private schools.[99] Nevertheless, the courts are prepared to sanction various forms of state aid where the benefits are primarily for the pupil rather than the school. Insofar as the federal Constitution is concerned, the Supreme Court can find no bar to state expenditure of tax funds for the purpose of supplying free textbooks to children in private sectarian as well as public schools.[100] State courts are divided on the question as to whether it is legally proper to furnish free bus transportation to parochial schools. It is considered proper in Maryland, for example, and improper in Wisconsin.[101] In 1947, though by a 5 to 4 vote, the Supreme Court ruled, on the basis of the child benefit theory, that Due Process does not forbid bus transportation to parochial schools at public expense.[102]

There are many "aids" to religion in this country at all levels of government. To mention but a few at the federal level, one might begin by observing that the very First Congress which wrote the First Amendment provided for chaplains in both Houses and in the armed services. There is compulsory chapel at the service academies, and religious services are held in federal hospitals and prisons. The President issues religious proclamations. The Bible is used for the administration of oaths. N.Y.A. and W.P.A. funds were available to parochial schools during the depression. Veterans receiving money under the "G.I." Bill of 1944 could attend denominational schools, to which payments were made directly by the government. During World War II, federal money was contributed to denominational schools for the training of nurses. The benefits of the National School Lunch Act are available to students in private as well as public schools. The Hospital Survey and Construction Act of 1946 specifically made money available to non-public hospitals. The slogan "In God We Trust" is used by the Treasury Department, and Congress recently added God to the pledge of allegiance. There is Bible-reading in

the schools of the District of Columbia, and religious instruction is given in the District's National Training
School for Boys. Religious organizations are exempt
from the federal income tax and are granted postal
privileges. Up to defined limits—15 per cent of the ad-
justed gross income of individuals and 5 per cent of the
net income of corporations—contributions to religious
organizations are deductible for federal income tax purposes. There are no limits to the deductibility of gifts
and bequests to religious institutions made under the
federal gift and estate tax laws.[103] This list of federal
"aids" could easily be expanded, and of course there is
a long list in each state.

6

We conclude, then, that in the nature of things neither
religious freedom nor the separation of church and state
can possibly be absolute. If Justice Vinson exaggerated
when he said that in modern society there are no absolutes at all, certainly he did not exaggerate very much.
Religious freedom must find its place in a constellation
of freedoms, and must often yield to interests which
under some circumstances have a claim to priority. And

a complete separation of all the affairs of the state from any and all aspects of religion is possible only in the fevered imaginations of fanatics.

Nevertheless, the essential relativity of the twin principles of religious freedom should not obscure the important fact that with us freedom and separation are the rule, and deviations from them the exceptions. The presumption is always on the side of freedom and separation, and therefore all doubts should be resolved in their favor. No one can spell out with any precision— not even the burgeoning behaviorists, at least not yet— the precise points at which religious freedom ends. I think all we can say is that where there is grave doubt, the restraint on religious freedom or the departure from separation had best be postponed or eschewed. Our tradition and prevailing values demand that we enjoy a maximum of religious freedom, and at least as much separation of church and state as religious freedom requires.

Should the United States Census Bureau ask people the question: "What is your religion?" The announced intention to ask the question in 1960 stirred up a considerable controversy, and I was delighted when the decision was reached in December, 1957, not to ask it. The question would have been an invasion of privacy, and would in effect have made the government an agent of religious groups. It would also have created a bad precedent, possibly leading to other encroachments on liberty. Should the courts enforce antenuptial agreements in mixed marriages relating to the religious upbringing of children? Since the observance of religious doctrine is a matter wholly of personal choice, the prevailing view in this country is that the writ of a civil court does not extend to such matters.[104]

Should sectarian instruction be available to public school children outside the school house, but on school time? I think the price we must pay for it is too high. It is bound to have an adverse psychological effect on nonparticipating children. Since the unreleased children cannot be given new work—for this would penalize the released—they must be content with mere busy work. Problems of safe and orderly dismissal, record-keeping and truancy are likely to be multiplied. Undesirable pressures on the children are inevitable, since many teachers are sorely tempted to become proselytizers for some sect. Thus there is the standing danger of creating new forms of religious intolerance. Finally, one may wonder whether it is wise in these days of so much earnest soul-searching about the adequacy of our educational system to reduce the amount of school time available for education in the regular curriculum. I should think that a much better case can be made for enlarging the school week than for shortening it. Should some sort of non-denominational religious instruction be given in the public schools? Let Reinhold Niebuhr answer the question: "There is probably no more ineffective way of teaching religion than to give an 'objective' account of religious history. For this means robbing the history of the inner meaning and of the specifically religious elements of faith and trust." [105]

In working out solutions for such questions as these, it is vital to remember what is the rule and what are at best exceptions to the rule. Our historic commitment is to religious freedom, the separation of church and state, secular public schools, secular government, and equal rights of religious conscience. We must never permit the exceptions to swallow up the rule.

2 *The Right to Communicate*

1

It is no exaggeration to say that from the point of view of constitutional law our American society is a free speech society. Freedom of speech has aptly been described as "the first freedom," [1] and some Justices of the Supreme Court, following a suggestion first put forward by Justice Stone in one of the most famous footnotes of legal history,[2] have taken the position that the right of free speech, together with the other First Amendment rights, enjoys a "preferred position" in our constitutional law. As Justice Stone observed, although a regulatory statute affecting ordinary commercial transactions carries with it the presumption of validity—he was talking about the validity of an act of Congress prohibiting the shipment of filled milk in interstate commerce— "there may be narrower scope for operation of the presumption of constitutionality when legislation appears on its face" to be contrary to specific constitutional rights, and particularly when the legislation "restricts those processes which can ordinarily be expected to bring about repeal of undesirable legislation. . . ." In such instances, he said, "more exacting judicial scrutiny" is in order than in the case of most other types of legislation.

The late Justices Rutledge [3] and Murphy expressed the belief that First Amendment freedoms have priority in our system of constitutional values; and of the present Justices, Black and Douglas are clearly committed to this position.[4] Not all the Justices, however, have accepted the preferred position doctrine, and it is not known whether a majority of the sitting Justices do so. Some have simply ignored it, and others, notably Justice Frankfurter, have actually rejected it. Thus Justice Frankfurter argued in the second flag salute case: [5] "There is no warrant in the constitutional basis of this Court's authority for attributing different roles to it depending upon the nature of the challenge to the legislation. Our power does not vary according to the particular provision of the Bill of Rights which is invoked."

Still later he complained that the phrase "preferred position of freedom of speech" had "uncritically crept into some recent opinions" of the Court, and he added: "I deem it a mischievous phrase, if it carries the thought, which it may subtly imply, that any law touching communication is infected with presumptive invalidity. . . . I say the phrase is mischievous because it radiates a constitutional doctrine without avowing it." [6]

Nevertheless, there is ample support for the view that while Justice Frankfurter may dislike the "preferred position" doctrine as an overly facile verbal formulation, he does agree that such First Amendment rights as freedom of speech go to the heart of the democratic process, and that judges must be especially alert when dealing with statutes which seem to invade these rights. Thus he said, in his concurring opinion in the Dennis case: [7] "In reviewing statutes which restrict freedoms protected by the First Amendment, we have emphasized the close relation which those freedoms bear to maintenance of a free society." Still later Justice Frankfurter declared: "For a citizen to be made to forego even a part of so basic a liberty as his political autonomy, the subordinating interest of the State must be compelling. . . . In the political realm, as in the academic, thought and action are presumptively immune from inquisition by political authority." [8] Finally, at the conclusion of a long review of free speech cases, Justice Frankfurter wrote: ". . . without freedom of expression, thought becomes checked and atrophied. Therefore, in considering what interests are so fundamental as to be enshrined in the Due Process Clause, those liberties of the individual which history has attested as the indispensable conditions of an open as against a closed society come to this Court with a momentum for respect lacking when appeal is made to liberties which derive merely from shifting economic arrangements." [9] To be sure, this is not "preferred position" language, but the underlying thought is about the same.

Indeed, it is quite inevitable that in any legal system which includes a number of constitutional rights, some rights will be given priority over others. For one thing, this is a logical necessity, since choices must often be made where one right collides with another. Furthermore, it is a fact of everyday experience that some rights matter more than others. For example, free speech is so vital to the very concept of democracy that it cannot be sacrificed without destroying democracy itself; but no one would really want to put such a high price on the Fifth Amendment right to grand jury indictment or the Second Amendment right to bear arms. The fact is that Great Britain, which was the original home of the grand jury indictment procedure, abandoned it in 1933 without impairing the edifice of justice; and everyone agrees that the right to bear arms must be kept within very narrow bounds for the safety of society.

The priority of some rights over others is a familiar fact of American legal history. Both James Madison and Thomas Jefferson graded the various guaranties and gave primacy to the First Amendment rights of freedom of religion and speech.[10] In the Insular Cases [11] following the Spanish-American War, the Supreme Court drew a distinction between fundamental and less-than-fundamental rights, and held that only the former followed the flag into our newly won colonial possessions. Similarly, in spelling out the content of the liberty which the Due Process Clause of the Fourteenth Amendment forbids the states to deny, the Supreme Court has consistently ruled that not all of the provisions of the federal Bill of Rights, but only those which are essential to justice, fall within the scope of the federal remedy.[12] Thus freedom of speech [13] and of the press,[14] and such procedural guarantees as the right to counsel,[15] have been incorporated into the great Civil War Amendment. On the other hand, the Court has ruled that due process does not embrace the right to a grand jury indictment,[16] or the Fifth Amendment protection against self-incrimination.[17] In other words, it is clear that in the jurisprudence of the Supreme Court, some rights are more important than others.

2

The case for free speech has been stated in classic language by some of the giant figures in the history of Western intellectual freedom. To mention only a few who spoke in our tongue, it was spelled out by Francis Bacon in 1605 in *The Advancement of Learning*, by John Milton in 1644 in his plea for unlicensed printing, *Areopagitica*, and much later in the modern idiom by John Stuart Mill in his essay *On Liberty*, published in 1859.[18] In our own day, the rationale for free speech has been spelled out by distinguished philosophers like Morris Raphael Cohen,[19] by such noted historians as Henry Steele Commager,[20] by such devoted legal scholars as Zechariah Chafee, Jr.,[21] and by thoughtful journalists.[22] But perhaps the most searching and eloquent statements of the case for free speech have in our times come from the Justices of the United States Supreme Court. These statements have the additional merits of being authoritative and of being responses to the solution of concrete problems arising in adversary litigation. They have not been emanations from some brooding omnipresence in the skies, for they rest upon specific human experiences. The method has been inductive rather than deductive, discrete rather than diffused.

It is incontestable that all of our Justices, whether "liberal" or "conservative," have been committed to the proposition that free speech is indispensable for our democracy, however much they may have differed in balancing competing interests in concrete cases. "Freedom of expression," Justice Frankfurter wrote in the Dennis case,[23] "is the well-spring of our civilization. . . ." For "the basis of the First Amendment," as Chief Justice Vinson explained in the same case, "is the hypothesis that speech can rebut speech, propaganda will answer propaganda, free debate of ideas will result in the wisest governmental policies. It is for this reason that this Court has recognized the inherent value of free discourse." [24] In his dissenting opinion in this case Justice Black said: "I have always believed that the First Amendment is the keystone of our Government, that the freedoms it guarantees provide the best insurance against destruction of all freedom." [25] And speaking in dissent also, Justice Douglas observed that "full and free discussion has indeed been the first article of our faith. We have founded our political system on it." [26] Thus, while the Justices split on the specific question of affirming or reversing the conviction of Dennis and his co-conspirators, all of them affirmed their belief in the primacy of freedom of speech.

From one point of view, the case for free speech rests upon the conviction that the best measure of truth is not necessarily the amount of force at the disposal of those who assert it. ". . . When men have realized," Justice Holmes once wrote in a memorable passage, "that time has upset many fighting faiths, they may come to believe even more than they believe the very foundations of their own conduct that the ultimate good desired is better reached by free trade in ideas— that the best test of truth is the power of the thought to get itself accepted in the competition of the market, and that truth is the only ground upon which their wishes safely can be carried out. That at any rate is the theory of our Constitution. It is an experiment, as all life is an experiment. Every year if not every day we have to wager our salvation upon some prophecy based upon imperfect knowledge." [27]

A free speech society is one in which political decisions are made only after free and open discussion; but this also means that after the decisions have been made, men are still at liberty to discuss them further and to urge their revocation or amendment according to some previously agreed-upon procedure. For freedom of speech rests upon the conviction that no one's particular truth, whether he is a public official or a private citizen, is such a final truth that it is not subject to criticism. "Truth and understanding," said John

Milton, "are not such wares as to be monopolised and traded in by tickets and statutes and standards. We must not think to make a staple commodity of all the knowledge in the land, to mark and license it like our broadcloth and our woolpacks." [28] The basic method of a free society is that of reaching essentially tentative conclusions, recognizing the contingent character of ideas and institutions. Accordingly, the rights which make up the substance of a free society describe a methodology for making and unmaking political decisions.

Free speech is built upon apprehensions concerning the use of power by those who control the enormous leviathan of our times, the state machinery. It is rooted in a profound skepticism about the nature of human nature.[29] Men cannot be trusted with power unless they first stand up to opposing candidates and different views in the free market place of democratic elections. Since public officials are not infallible, their opinions and decisions, in the nature of things, do not have the quality of final truth. Thus free speech is a guaranty of the free expression of conflicting opinions. In the political field it means that no majority ever has a permanent claim to power. Since free speech protects the right to disagree with those who happen to be in power for the moment, it denies the legitimacy of either permanent or absolute power. It assumes the fallibility of all men, including the most powerful public officials. It recognizes that political power is such a corrupting force in society that it cannot be permitted to go unchecked.

In a larger sense, the Justices of the Supreme Court have often noted, freedom of speech is indispensable for progress. "When ideas compete in the market for acceptance," Justice Douglas said recently, "full and free discussion exposes the false and they gain few adherents. Full and free discussion even of ideas we hate encourages the testing of our own prejudices and preconceptions. Full and free discussion keeps a society from becoming stagnant and unprepared for the stresses and strains that work to tear all civilizations apart." [30] For, as Justice Brandeis once asserted: "Those who won our independence by revolution were not cowards. They did not fear political change." [31] It is imperative, Chief Justice Hughes wrote in 1937, "to preserve inviolate the constitutional rights of free speech, free press and free assembly in order to maintain the opportunity for free political discussion, to the end that government may be responsive to the will of the people and that changes, if desired, may be obtained by peaceful means. Therein lies the security of the Republic, the very foundation of constitutional government." [32] Thus, however trite it may be to say it once more, free speech is not a counsel of weakness. A government of limited powers, Justice Jackson said in the second flag salute case, "need not be anemic government. Assurance that rights are secure tends to diminish fear and jealousy of strong government, and by making us feel safe to live under it makes for its better support." [33]

3

Two members of the present Court, Justices Black and Douglas, seem to take a fairly absolutist position with regard to freedom of speech.[34] An occasional philosophical writer, such as Alexander Meiklejohn, reads the First Amendment as "an absolute, unqualified prohibition." [35] But even Meiklejohn is not to be taken quite so literally as he seems to take the First Amendment, for he is quick to recognize the legitimacy of forbidding libelous and slanderous words, or words inciting men to crime, or sedition and treason expressed in speech and writing. He satisfies his own instinct for consistency by explaining that the First Amendment does not forbid the abridging of speech, but only the abridging of the freedom of speech.[36] Thus Meiklejohn manages to eat his cake and have it at the same time, a miracle beyond the capacity of most ordinary mortals who are deficient in the talent for sentence-squeezing.

At the other extreme, of course, are the people who

reject, more or less, the whole concept of free speech. Thus a young scholar rcently wrote a book to argue that the Court should construe the First Amendment, not to safeguard freedom primarily, but to promote morality and virtue—justice and not freedom being "the central political virtue." [37] If, as he argues, the right to speak extends only to the speaking of the right things, I shall have to suspend any serious judgment concerning the merits of his thesis until he gets around to explaining what is right and what is wrong. Since this problem was wrestled with by such philosophical and moral luminaries as Isaiah and Jeremiah, Plato and Aristotle, St. Augustine and St. Thomas, Gautama Buddha, Confucius, and Bertrand Russell, I await the word of this latter-day apostle of virtue and justice with considerable interest. It may well turn out that there is a lot of truth in the observation that "the books are balanced in heaven, not here."

Most reasonable people, including most judges, seek to balance their books here, as best they may; and however much they may prize freedom of speech, they decline to believe that it is never legitimate to recognize limits upon that freedom. Surely few people have cared more about free speech than Justice Holmes, and yet he wrote, in the very midst of the post-World War I "red scare," [38] that "the First Amendment while prohibiting legislation against free speech as such cannot have been, and obviously was not, intended to give immunity for every possible use of language." [39] And by way of specific illustration, Justice Holmes added: "We venture to believe that neither Hamilton nor Madison, nor any other competent person then or later, ever supposed that to make criminal the counseling of a murder within the jurisdiction of Congress would be an unconstitutional interference with free speech." It is of interest that at the very beginning of his influential book on free speech—perhaps still the best book we have on this subject—the late Professor Chafee made this point in his characteristically direct way when he said: "This book . . . is in no way an argument that any one should be allowed to say whatever he wants anywhere and at any time. We can all agree from the very start that there must be some point where the government may step in. . . ." [40]

In fact, almost all state constitutional guaranties of freedom of speech and press warn against the abuse of this freedom. Thus the Constitution of Alabama declares that "any person may speak, write and publish his sentiments on all subjects, being responsible for the abuse of that liberty." [41] The most explicit of all state constitutional provisions on this point is that of West Virginia, which states: "No law abridging the freedom of speech, or of the press, shall be passed; but the Legislature may, by suitable penalties, restrain the publication or sale of obscene books, papers or pictures, and provide for the punishment of libel, and defamation of character, and for the recovery, in civil actions, by the aggrieved party, of suitable damages for such libel, or defamation." [42]

4

Since a man is legally liable under our law for his harmful acts, and since words as well as physical acts may do harm, it follows that the utterance of words may under a variety of circumstances be actionable or punishable. Just as an assault or battery may do harm to the body, so does a libel or slander do harm to reputation, with the protection of which the law is very much concerned. There are few indeed in the English-speaking world who are not aware of those famous lines from *Othello*:

"Good name in man and woman, dear my lord,
  Is the immediate jewel of their souls;
  Who steals my purse steals trash; 'tis something,
    nothing;
  'Twas mine, 'tis his, and has been slave to thousands;
  But he that filches from me my good name
  Robs me of that which not enriches him,
  And makes me poor indeed."

In many circumstances words are acts, and often the only acts that may be involved. Thus, one who takes the money of another under false pretenses or by means of a fraud cannot set up the constitutional defense that all he used were words, since the words alone constitute the offense. All sorts of statutes are concerned with words, such as statutes forbidding false advertising, misbranding, or mislabeling; and the law has long recognized liability for negligent words.[43] Incitement to crime is punishable, even though words alone were utilized by the wrong-doer.

Certainly the most familiar and the most widely recognized limitation on free speech is found in the law of libel and slander.[44] The authors of the First Amendment were well aware that at the common law libel and slander were actionable wrongs and that libel could be a crime as well. No Justice of the Supreme Court, however absolutist his position on free speech, has ever so much as hinted that the law of defamation was constitutionally improper. In the law today, "a communication is defamatory if it tends so to harm the reputation of another as to lower him in the estimation of the community or to deter third persons from associating or dealing with him." [45] At the common law, the truth was a complete defense to a libel action, but many state constitutions add that the utterance must in addition have been made for "good and justifiable ends." [46] In addition, it is an adequate defense that the publication is a fair and accurate report of a public proceeding, such as a court trial or a legislative debate. A statement of facts which affects an important interest of the recipient of the communication, such as a statement to a prospective employer regarding a person seeking employment, if made by one who honestly and reasonably believed it to be true, is not actionable even if mistaken. Otherwise employers would have a difficult time trying to find out the facts they are entitled to have. But it is important to note that malice makes a difference. For example, a false and defamatory communication to an FBI agent, if made with malice, is not privileged; and the giving of such a communication is actionable.[47]

Another recognized defense to a libel action is that of fair comment, such as criticism of a book or place. "Every man who publishes a book," Lord Ellenborough wrote over a century and a half ago, "commits himself to the judgment of the public, and anyone may comment upon his performance. If the commentator does not step aside from the work, or introduce fiction for the purpose of condemnation, he exercises a fair and legitimate right. . . . The critic does a great service to the public, who writes down any vapid or useless publication such as ought never to have appeared. He checks the dissemination of bad taste, and prevents people from wasting both their time and money upon trash." [48] Similarly, one who holds or seeks a public office is subject to "legitimate criticism" in the newspapers.[49] But criticism of activities which are a matter of public concern is privileged, although defamatory, only if based upon a true statement of fact which represents the actual opinion of the critic and which was not made solely for the purpose of causing harm.[50] Since public criticism reaches more people than most ordinary communications, it must at least be right on the facts.

The law of libel and slander stands, then, as a warning that freedom of speech does not mean that we are free to say anything we want to say, to anyone, at any time. Our society values very highly the right to communicate ideas freely, but it also values the right to a good reputation. Thus the New York Court of Appeals held in 1947 that calling a person a Communist, in the light of present-day public aversion to Communism, is libelous per se.[51] The Court said that whether a writing is defamatory depends, among other things, upon "the temper of the times, the current of contemporary public opinion," and that it is therefore no answer that Communists are permitted to function as a political party. In fact, American courts are almost unanimous in holding that it is libelous per se falsely to impute that one is a Communist, since "the law assumes that anyone called a

Communist suffers serious damage to reputation." [52] As a federal court of appeals said a few years ago, the label of Communism today, "in the minds of many average and respectable persons," places the individual so labeled "beyond the pale of respectability." [53] Similarly, several courts held soon after World War II that a charge that one was a Nazi or pro-Nazi was actionable.[54] However, since members of Congress are constitutionally immune from lawsuits for anything said in the course of their official duties, there is at present no legal protection against defamation emanating from this source.[55]

Under the general law of defamation, individuals, business enterprises, and fairly small identifiable groups may sue; or defamation in such cases may be prosecuted in the criminal courts. Where a very large group is defamed—such as all Negroes of a big city—no individual member of the group has a right to sue for damages, and ordinarily no action for criminal libel may be brought. But the German experience under Hitler drew attention to the serious consequences of rampant group vilification, to the fact that the defamation of large groups can be a cruel and destructive instrument of political power. Accordingly, some states have tried their hand with group libel laws, and Congress has often been urged to bar false propaganda defaming religious or racial groups from the mails.[56] Such statutes, however, raise grave constitutional questions, particularly statutes with criminal sanctions against class defamation.[57]

The New Jersey legislature enacted a "race hatred" law in 1935, but the highest court of the state held it unconstitutional in 1941 as being too vague and indefinite and as an impairment of freedom of speech.[58] Three members of the German-American Bund had made scurrilous attacks upon Jews in public speeches. The statute forbade public speeches which incited, counseled, promoted, or advocated "hatred, abuse, violence or hostility against any group or groups of persons residing" in the state "by reason of race, color, religion or manner of worship."

The state of Illinois, however, has an older statute on this subject, dating from 1917, which makes it a crime to sell, advertise, publish, or exhibit in public any lithograph, moving picture, or play which "portrays depravity, criminality, unchastity or lack of virtue of a class of citizens, of any race, color, creed or religion," where the publication or exhibition exposes members of the vilified groups to "contempt, derision or obloquy," or produces a breach of the peace or riots. A few years ago, this statute was put to the test when the founder, director, and president of an organization in Chicago called the "White Circle League of America" distributed a paper which charged Negroes, in inflammatory language, with all sorts of evil things—aggressions, rapes, robberies, drug addiction, use of weapons, and the like. In 1951 the highest court of Illinois held the statute valid, mainly on the ground that it was reasonable to anticipate that such libelous language was likely to result in violence and disorder between the races.[59] The following year, though dividing 5 to 4, the Supreme Court of the United States affirmed,[60] treating the state statute, as the state court did, as a criminal libel law designed to prohibit words liable to cause violence and disorder.

Speaking for the Court, Justice Frankfurter said that there was plenty of evidence, here and abroad, to give warrant to the state's view "that wilful purveyors of falsehood concerning racial and religious groups promote strife and tend powerfully to obstruct the manifold adjustments required for free, ordered life in a metropolitan, polygot community."[61] As for the argument that legislation is not helpful in this area, the Justice said that in the absence of confident solutions for the problem, the judiciary should not deny the legislature any reasonable choice of policy. It would be "arrant dogmatism," he asserted, for the Court to say that a state legislature may not believe that a man's position may depend as much on the reputation of the racial or religious group to which he belongs as upon his own merits. Finally, the Court did not even consider the "clear and present danger" standard, because libelous utterances are not within the area of constitutionally protected speech to begin with.

Each of the four dissenters in this case filed his own opinion. Justice Black protested that the decision degraded First Amendment freedoms and left them almost completely at the mercy of state governments. He insisted "that no legislature is charged with the duty or vested with the power to decide what public issues Americans can discuss. In a free country, that is the individual's choice, not the state's." [62] He added that sugar-coating a censorship law by calling it a group libel law may make it more palatable, but it is no less deadly. Justice Reed argued that the statute was unconstitutionally vague because some of its key words, such as "virtue," "derision," and "obloquy," were too vague for a criminal statute. Justice Douglas stressed the importance of giving First Amendment rights a preferred position, arguing that these rights "are above and beyond the police power; they are not subject to regulation in the manner of factories, slums, apartment houses, production of oil, and the like." [63] Finally, Justice Jackson, in his dissenting opinion, maintained that the state statute, as applied in this case, dispensed with accepted safeguards for the accused, such as the right to offer proof to the jury regarding the truth of his publication or regarding his motives in preparing it. State libel laws, Justice Jackson maintained, are not a threat to a free press only where there are adequate safeguards: the right to have a jury decide both law and fact, the defense of truth, and the "clear and present danger" rule.

Although there have been a few successful prosecutions for group defamation under ordinary criminal libel laws,[64] generally speaking, these laws apply only where an identifiable individual has been injured.[65] A very small number of states, in addition to Illinois, now have group libel laws.[66] An Indiana statute proscribes "racketeering in hatred"; [67] a Massachusetts law makes it illegal to "maliciously promote hatred of any group . . . because of race, color or religion"; [68] a Nevada statute declares it to be an offense "to impeach the honesty, integrity, virtue, or reputation, or to publish the natural defects, of . . . [a] community of persons"; [69] a Connecticut statute forbids group defamation by advertisements; [70] a West Virginia statute outlaws defamation of any race or class of citizens by theatricals or pictures; [71] and New Mexico forbids the publication of defamatory statements about religious societies and fraternal orders.[72] A few large cities also have ordinances which make unlawful the engendering of race or religious hatred.[73]

Though at least one well-known state group libel law

has cleared the hurdle of Supreme Court review—by the barest possible margin—it cannot be said that all the constitutional questions have been settled. Above all, a criminal statute must give potential offenders adequate notice of just what conduct is forbidden, and on this score some of the group libel laws are extremely vulnerable. Furthermore, wholly apart from questions of constitutional law, group libel legislation is open to serious objections. It may tend to discourage the processes of open discussion, and involve the courts, as in the case of the libeling of religious groups, in becoming arbiters of religious truth. Furthermore, there is the danger that if a group libel law is limited to racial and religious groups, as is usually done, other groups will demand the same protection. Why not? "If Jehovah's Witnesses must never be slurred," Professor Chafee once asked, "why should the CIO or savings banks or co-operatives or railroads submit to unwarranted vilification without any redress?" [74]

In the absence of much experience with group libel laws, one may speculate on how well they will work. They may lead to frequent and complicated litigation. These statutes are vaguely worded of necessity, and just what constitutes truth in describing large groups will be difficult to describe. Much, perhaps too much, will depend upon the prejudices of prosecutors and jurors; and if it be objected that such prejudices already play a large role in the administration of justice, a short answer may well be that it is unwise knowingly to give prejudice a longer leash than it already has. It is also doubtful if much is gained through a criminal trial; for if the vilifier is acquitted, he can say he has some sort of official approval for his activities, and if he is convicted, he may achieve martyrdom. In addition, there is the danger that prosecutions for group libel will increase group tensions, with group prejudice coming to a sharp focus in litigation. Finally, as Professor Chafee suggested, group vilification is a symptom of evils which group libel laws cannot reach. "The less one can say publicly, the more he will say in private. The very suppression of publications and meetings is made a fresh cause for hatred of the opposing group, which is accused of controlling the officials who do the suppressing." [75] Whether these results will necessarily follow we do not know, but it is of interest to note that such groups as President Truman's Committee on Civil Rights, the American Civil Liberties Union, the Anti-Defamation League, and the Commission on the Freedom of the Press have been opposed to group libel legislation, and prefer to use extralegal methods of education, conciliation, persuasion and discussion.[76] They believe, in short, that ordinarily the most effective remedy for bad speech is good speech.

5

Defamation is, of course, only one of many illustrations of the concerns of our society which set limits to the freedom of speech. Any going system has a tremendous stake in maintaining orderly social relations and in avoiding incitements to violence, criminality, and breaches of the peace. To be sure, the Supreme Court is willing to go a long way before recognizing the validity of a restriction upon speech. Thus in the well-known case of *Terminiello* v. *Chicago*,[77] decided in 1949, the Court reversed the conviction of a vicious rabble-rouser because the trial judge had defined the statutory "breach of the peace" as misbehavior which "stirs the public to anger, invites dispute, brings about a condition of unrest," and so on. Speaking for a bare majority of the Court, Justice Douglas said that "a function of free speech under our system of government is to invite dispute. It may indeed best serve its high purpose when it induces a condition of unrest, creates dissatisfaction with conditions as they are, or even stirs people to anger. Speech is often provocative and challenging." [78]

But speech is often more than that; and of the four

dissenting Justices, three thought that Terminiello's case fell within the scope of the "fighting words" doctrine, which excludes from the area of constitutionally protected speech, abusive and insulting utterances which may lead to breaches of the peace. Justice Jackson severely criticized the Court for holding to "a conception of freedom of speech so rigid as to tolerate no concession to society's need for public order." [79] He warned that the Court's decision was lending aid and comfort to both left and right wing extremist totalitarians who seek only to discredit democratic authority in their battle for control of the streets. He would go far in recognizing the power of cities and states to keep their streets from becoming the battleground of hostile ideologies. And he concluded: "In the long run, maintenance of free speech will be more endangered if the population can have no protection from the abuses which lead to violence. No liberty is made more secure by holding that its abuses are inseparable from its enjoyment. . . . The choice is not between order and liberty. It is between liberty with order and anarchy without either." [80]

The Terminiello decision actually turned on the fact that the trial judge used an inept phrase in instructing the jury on the law of free speech. Only a few years earlier, the Court had ruled unanimously that the prevention and punishment of one who utters insulting or "fighting" words in public have never been thought to raise any constitutional problems.[81] The right to curse a public officer on the streets, the Court held, must yield to the social interest in order and morality. Justice Murphy, one of the most devoted believers in free speech, spoke for the Court, and said flatly that "it is well understood that the right of free speech is not absolute at all times and under all circumstances." The use of such epithets as "damned racketeer" and "damned Fascist," he declared, is likely to provoke the average person to retaliation and thus cause a breach of the peace. Similarly, the Court ruled unanimously in the same year that in contrast with the communication of information and opinion, the Constitution imposes no restraints insofar as purely commercial advertising is concerned.[82] The extent to which the use of the streets for the pursuit of a gainful occupation is in derogation of public interests was held to be a matter of legislative judgment.

The interests of the state in the public uses of streets and parks are very great, and the police are conceded to have a proper discretionary power to interfere with a street meeting if necessary to preserve order and protect the general welfare.[83] The police cannot forbid the expression of unpopular views, the Court has ruled; but where the speaker passes the bounds of argument and persuasion and incites to riot, the police are not at all powerless to prevent a breach of the peace. Although cities may go far in controlling the use of parks and streets by speakers through non-discriminatory licensing devices,[84] the Court has insisted, however, that the right to hold meetings in such public places cannot be made to depend upon the undefined and unrestrained discretion of administrative officials.[85] The discretion of the licensing officials must be controlled by "narrowly drawn, reasonable and definite standards"; for the right of free speech must have "a firmer foundation than the whims or personal opinions of a local governing body." [86] Furthermore, a city goes too far if it prohibits the distribution of handbills on the streets altogether,[87] or forbids speech in public parks.[88] Regulation, yes, prohibition, no.

Similarly, the Court ruled in 1943 that a city may not forbid Jehovah's Witnesses to ring doorbells or knock on doors for the purpose of handing out religious literature; [89] but a few years later it upheld, in a case involving magazine solicitors, a Green River ordinance which forbade door-to-door solicitation of orders for the sale of goods without the prior consent of the occupants.[90] The presence or absence of the commercial element was regarded as the decisive factor.

Roughly comparable results were reached in cases dealing with the use of loud-speakers on the streets. When the Court first faced this problem, in 1948, it held, though by a 5 to 4 vote, that a city ordinance which forbids the use of loud-speakers altogether, except in the uncontrolled discretion of the chief of police, was unconstitutional on its face as a previous restraint on free speech.[91] It was noted that today loud-speakers are "indispensable instruments of effective public speech." The protest of the dissenters that cities have a right to make city life more endurable was not really in vain, however; for the following year, though again by a 5 to 4 vote, the Court upheld an ordinance which forbade any sound truck or loud-speaker "which emits . . . loud and raucous noises." [92] Although municipalities may not forbid all use of loud-speakers, Justice Reed declared, unrestrained use of all sound-amplifying devices throughout a municipality would be intolerable; and he held that the ordinance in question was merely regulatory, and designed to protect the citizen's claim to comfort and convenience. As Justice Frankfurter observed in a concurring opinion, the state may protect man from "aural aggressions." Since loud-speakers which do not emit loud and raucous noises are not doing what they are supposed to do, there is a great deal of merit in the view of the dissenters that the two loud-speaker decisions cannot be reconciled with each other. Certainly cities now exercise a wide latitude of judgment in dealing with the problems presented by the use of sound-amplifying devices in public places.[93]

Still another area of communication where the Court

has found it essential to recognize serious limits to freedom of expression is that of picketing. In 1940 the Court ruled squarely in the Thornhill case [94] that a state statute forbidding all picketing, carried on for any purpose and whether of a peaceful character or not, was an unconstitutional abridgment of free speech. Justice Murphy said that freedom of speech "embraces at least the liberty to discuss publicly and truthfully all matters of public concern without previous restraint or fear of subsequent punishment," and that "in the circumstances of our times the dissemination of information concerning the facts of a labor dispute must be regarded as within that area of free discussion that is guaranteed by the Constitution." At the same time the Court also invalidated a municipal ordinance which made it unlawful for any person to carry or display any sign or banner in connection with picketing, on the ground that it interfered with "a natural and appropriate means of conveying information on matters of public concern." [95] A bit later on, the Court extended the scope of the Thornhill doctrine to include "stranger" picketing,[96] and held that there need not be a "labor dispute" within the definition of state law for a union to enjoy the Fourteenth Amendment right to express a grievance by means of picketing.[97]

Though the Court has never receded from the position that picketing is a way of communicating ideas and therefore falls within the constitutional guaranty of free speech, it quickly became apparent that it might involve more than speech. Many years and many cases after Thornhill, so devoted a friend of freedom of expression as Justice Douglas conceded that "of course, we have always recognized that picketing has aspects which make it more than speech." [98] Thus the Court held, soon after Thornhill, that if the picketing was carried on in a context of violence, the state may enjoin not only the acts of violence but the picketing as well, since the state may justifiably conclude that the momentum of fear generated by past violence might survive.[99] By a 5 to 4 vote the Court also ruled that a state may, under its police power, localize industrial conflict by prohibiting the picketing of a business wholly outside the context of the real dispute, on the theory that a state may forbid the "conscription of neutrals." [100] But the most serious restraints upon picketing have resulted from the Court's elaboration of the proposition that a state may forbid peaceful picketing where the picketing is conducted for a purpose properly made illegal under state law.

In the first important case on this subject, decided in 1949, a unanimous Court ruled that a state may enjoin peaceful picketing designed to accomplish a purpose forbidden by the state anti-trade-restraint statute.[101] The Court held that constitutional guarantees of free speech do not give labor a peculiar immunity from laws against trade-restraint combinations which are denied to all other people. It was noted that the Court had never decided a case which asserts "a constitutional right in picketers to take advantage of speech or press to violate valid laws designed to protect important interests of society."

Soon afterward, the Court also held that it was immaterial whether the statute which the picketing violated is buttressed by criminal or civil sanctions, this being entirely a matter of state policy.[102] In fact, it also ruled, in the same year, that the rule applies even where the public policy of the state is determined by the courts rather than by the legislature.[103] Since the Fourteenth Amendment leaves the states free to distribute the powers of government between their legislative and judicial branches as they please, it does not matter that the illegal purpose is defined by judges rather than by legislators. Although picketing is a mode of communication, it is inseparably something more, Justice Frankfurter argued, and therefore "picketing is not beyond the control of a State if the manner in which picketing is conducted or the purposes which it seeks to effectuate gives ground for its disallowance." [104] It is now clearly established in American law that picketing is more than the mere communication of ideas, that it cannot be immune from all state regulation, and that courts must weigh in the balance competing interests of public policy.[105] Picketing may be forbidden if its purpose is to pursue an objective made unlawful by state or federal law. It follows that the Thornhill rule, which was announced in 1940, has already practically sunk from view under a great weight of exceptions.

6

It is a familiar principle of American public law that the freedoms of speech and press do not extend to obscene utterances. There are many laws in the federal statute books and in those of all the states which penalize obscenity.[106] It is difficult to explain just why our society is so concerned with obscenity; but whatever the reasons may be, the concern exists and finds expression in penal laws. In fact, in a recent full-dress review of the whole problem, the Supreme Court noted that "the rejection of obscenity as utterly without redeeming social importance" is not only an American but a universal judgment; and the Court squarely ruled that it is not within the area of constitutionally protected speech or press.[107]

It is deceptively easy, however, to say that obscenity is beyond the legal pale. The hard questions are: First, how is obscenity to be defined? and second, who is to make the decision, and according to what procedure? It goes without saying that mere bad taste, or vulgarity, or even nudity, is not the legal measure of obscenity. As Justice Voelker of the Supreme Court of Michigan pointed out in a very recent decision which held that the members of a private nudist colony were not guilty of the offense of indecent exposure, "private fanaticism or even bad taste is not yet ground for police interference. If eccentricity were a crime then all of us were felons." [108] Arguing that nudity is not necessarily synonymous with indecency, Justice Voelker said: "If this assumption were valid few artists could continue to work from live models, or, veering somewhat to a related field, the curators of our art galleries and museums would have to turn to the cultivation of fig leaves; and that stalwart badge of middle-class respectability, the *National Geographic Magazine,* would be banished from the hearth to the censor's shears." [109] To prove indecent exposure, the Michigan Court ruled, the state must show, first, that the exposer had an indecent intention, and, second, "a reasonably-to-be-expected reaction of shock and outrage by the probable or potential exposees." [110] As to this the Court said: "Guilt or innocence of indecent exposure is not a matter of measuring the amount of human flesh exposed; one does not caliper the revealed epidermis and certify guilt as increasing by the square inch; the indecency of an exposure is always a matter of intent to be gathered from all the circumstances." [111]

The law in this country on the subject of obscene utterances, oral and written, has at long last come to a position like that taken by the Michigan Court with reference to indecent exposure. In reaching this point our courts had to abandon the old common law rule, which received its classic formulation in Chief Justice Cockburn's opinion in the landmark Hicklin case, decided in 1868.[112] ". . . I think," he wrote, "the test of obscenity is this, whether the tendency of the matter charged as obscenity is to deprave and corrupt those whose minds are open to such immoral influences, and into whose hands a publication of this sort may fall." Obviously the major objection to this test is that the standard for the public's reading matter is geared to the most suggestible psyche or the feeblest mind in the community.

This test was rejected in 1933 by Federal Judge John Woolsey in the case involving the importation of James Joyce's *Ulysses*.[113] After all, there are terribly wide differences among people in such matters. As Judge Curtis Bok of the Court of Quarter Sessions of Philadelphia County observed in a famous opinion on this subject, the Hicklin rule, if applied strictly, "renders any book unsafe, since a moron could pervert to some sexual fantasy to which his mind is open the listings in a seed catalogue." [114] In fact, Judge Bok went on to point out that even average, normal people react differently to the printed page, depending upon changing moods. "If he reads an obscene book when his sensuality is low," he wrote, "he will yawn over it or find that its suggestibility leads him off on quite different paths. If he reads the Mechanics' Lien Act while his sensuality is high, things will stand between him and the page that have no business there." [115]

There have been other attempts to define obscenity. Many strictly legal definitions do not help at all. As a matter of law, obscene means lewd or lascivious; but if you look up the definition of lewd, you will find that it means obscene or lascivious, and what does lascivious mean? You've guessed it: it means obscene or lewd. This sort of inquiry is not very fruitful. It is very difficult to get a really adequate legal definition of obscenity, because, as Zechariah Chafee, Jr., once pointed out, the law likes to be logical, whereas sex is largely irrational; the law seeks to define and protect a common standard, whereas in the field of sex there seems to be an extraordinary lack of consensus.[116] In fact, the concern with obscenity takes vastly different forms with different people. Some object to obscenity merely on grounds of offensiveness; some oppose obscenity ideologically in order to protect accepted moral standards from criticism; still others fear obscenity because they are apprehensive that it may lead to immoral conduct through the stimulation of sexual impulses and impure thoughts. A writer once ventured to define obscene as that which "rouses to genital commotion." But we could not possibly live with such a test. For one thing, it would destroy the advertising business. I suppose back-rubs and perfumes would also have to go. And what are we to do about Kinsey's discovery that sitting in hot sand leads to genital commotion?

Of course, one can always find people, including judges, who believe that one can tell instinctively whether a book is obscene.[117] A brief look into the history of obscenity ought to be sufficient to dispel this notion, for many books now regarded as perfectly proper were once barred as unclean, including such classics as Swift's *Gulliver's Travels,* Charlotte Brontë's *Jane Eyre,* Richardson's *Pamela,* Hawthorne's *Scarlet Letter,* Eliot's *Adam Bede,* and Hardy's *Tess.* Books by such great authors as Whitman, Montaigne, Sterne, Balzac, Hugo, Flaubert, and Mark Twain ran into all sorts of censorship difficulties.[118] The changeableness of taste in such matters should give one pause in asserting any instinctive standard of judgment. In Comstock's heyday, the Kinsey books would have been confiscated on sight; today they are regarded as quite innocuous and even mildly informative.

The rejection of the Hicklin rule was spelled out by the United States Supreme Court on February 25, 1957, in the case of *Butler* v. *Michigan.*[119] Butler had been convicted of selling a paperback book in violation of a Michigan statute which defined as obscene any publication which might tend "to incite minors to violent or depraved or immoral acts," or which might tend "to the corruption of the morals of youth." The Supreme Court set aside the conviction by unanimous vote, Justice Frankfurter saying: "The State insists that, by thus quarantining the general reading public against books not too rugged for grown men and women in order to shield juvenile innocence, it is exercising its power to promote the general welfare. Surely, this is to burn the house to roast the pig. . . . We have before us legislation not reasonably restricted to the evil with which it is said to deal. The incidence of this enactment is to reduce the adult population of Michigan to reading only what is fit for children. It thereby arbitrarily curtails one of those liberties of the individual, now enshrined in the Due Process Clause of the Fourteenth Amendment, that history has attested as the indispensable conditions for the maintenance and progress of a free society."

Finally, on June 24, 1957, in *Roth* v. *United States*,[120] the Supreme Court reviewed the whole problem of legislative control of publications alleged to be obscene. Speaking for the Court, Justice Brennan noted that the Court had always assumed that obscenity is not protected by the constitutional guaranty of freedom of speech and press. He then proceeded to define obscene material as "material which deals with sex in a manner appealing to prurient interest." In a footnote, he explained, "i.e., material having a tendency to excite lustful thoughts." [121] But as Justice Harlan pointed out in his dissenting opinion, there is a great deal of difference between "appealing to prurient interests," and "exciting lustful thoughts." And he added that the latter test is "unrealistically broad for a society that plainly tolerates a great deal of erotic interest in literature, advertising and art. . . ." [122] Justice Harlan complained that the Court had merely assimilated the various definitions "into one indiscriminate potpourri." It should also be observed that adding the word "prurient" to the older words, such as obscene, lewd and lascivious, hardly contributes very much to a clarification of the problem. This seems to be another attempt to define the indefinable.

Although the convictions that were appealed from were sustained in the Roth case, and both federal and state laws forbidding obscene literature were held constitutional, the enduring significance of the decision lies in the effort to keep the thrust of the Court's ruling within reasonable boundaries. Justice Brennan made it clear that sex and obscenity are not synonymous; that the portrayal of sex in art and literature is not in itself bad; that sex is one of man's vital problems and has always been one of his most absorbing interests—as any eavesdropper on almost any undergraduate conversation will learn in ten minutes; that a publication should not be judged on the basis of isolated passages alone; and, above all, that the test of obscenity is not the possible effect of the material upon particularly suggestible people. In contrast with the Hicklin rule, said Justice Brennan, the American test is "whether to the average person, applying contemporary community standards, the dominant theme of the material taken as a whole appeals to prurient interests." [123] In fact, the Hicklin rule was specifically rejected as being unconstitutionally restrictive of the freedoms of speech and press.

Concurring separately, Chief Justice Warren and Justice Harlan protested that the language of the majority opinion was much too broad. Justices Douglas and Black dissented on the theory that the test adopted by the Court gives the censor "free range over a vast domain." Justice Douglas warned that "the test that suppresses a cheap tract today can suppress a literary gem tomorrow," [124] and urged that we should have confidence in the ability of our people to reject noxious literature.

Although the Court sustained several convictions under both state and federal laws in the spring of 1957,[125] it quickly became apparent that the Court did not by any means issue a blank check to the censors. For in the following Term the Court set aside several convictions of publishers of nudist magazines and other publications, citing the Roth case in each instance as authority.[126] The many safeguards spelled out in the Roth opinion are likely to be far more important for the future of literary censorship than the attempt at a substantive definition of something which defies definition.

7

We have a tremendous stake in protecting the free exercise of the right to communicate. It is the hallmark of our open society. But freedom of speech does not exist except in a social context, and in this context other things also count for a great deal. The right to speak one's mind must often yield to our concern for reputation and for public order. The right to communicate in the streets, parks, and other public places must be exercised with due regard for the convenience of the public. Picketing is a legitimate way of communicating ideas, but it may not be exercised to accomplish unlawful ends. Those who publish must respect the community's moral sensibilities with regard to what is obscene, lewd, lascivious, or prurient.

There is no simple or single verbal device which will pull these legitimate limitations on free speech together into a ready formula. This branch of our constitutional law—like all others—is a product of experience, reason, tradition, and the pushing and hauling of competing social interests. Many factors go into the cauldron of final judgment: our religious teachings, our legal and political principles, our philosophies, the imperatives of the economy, the views of our sainted ancestors, and, I suppose above all else, what our mothers taught us.

3 *The Right to Talk Politics*

1

I have often speculated whether it is sufficiently understood that the politics of a free country is psychically disturbing. Where law and order under efficient government exist, aggressive, violent conduct on the physical plane between man and man and between groups, for the resolution of differences, is effectively forbidden. I suppose the most elemental function of government is to rule out the use of force as a method for settling disputes between men. But since, in any social system, the differences and the disputes persist anyhow, instead of resorting to physical violence, men turn to verbal violence. It is a sort of inevitable sublimation. And the only truth in the old adage that "sticks and stones may break my bones, but words can't hurt me," is that the sticks and stones hurt more, and the words, in comparison, less, though there are probably many exceptions even to this proposition. In a state of civilization, everyone must know that words can hurt very deeply indeed. Furthermore, words often bring on the sticks and stones.

Not only does verbal violence take the place of physical violence, where the latter is suppressed through the agency of effective government, but in free countries the very existence of the guaranty of freedom of speech offers assurance that there will be a great deal of verbal aggression. The very essence of free government is that on all matters of opinion men are perfectly at liberty to differ. Above all else, they are free to differ with those in power. The right to talk politics includes the right to talk against those who for the moment hold the power of government in their hands.

The hallmark of democratic government is that criticism and opposition to the party in office are perfectly legitimate. In fact, the system cannot function properly without opposition and criticism. The most important single security against the abuse of power in democratic systems is the availability of an opposition party ready and eager to take over the reins of authority. But opposition would be ineffective in any constitutional sense unless the opposition is assured those rights which make opposition meaningful. These include, as a bare minimum, the right to speak freely and critically about those in power, the right to present candidates for public office in honestly conducted elections, and the right of free association. It goes to the heart of the matter that organized, vigorous opposition to those in power is not evidence of treason or sedition.

In democratic societies, allegiance is due, not to the party in power or to its leaders, but to the state itself, the whole political organism. It is fundamental in democratic political theory and constitutional law that we distinguish between the state and the government, which is only the servant of the state, and between the state, the government, and the party in power. No party in a democracy has a permanent claim to power. A party must win office in a free political contest in which an opposing party or parties are free to compete on the same legal terms. Those who oppose the men who for the time being occupy the public offices perform an indispensable service, without which freedom itself would be a mere sham. That is why the opposition function is legally and morally legitimate. "It is the highest achievement of democratic societies," Reinhold Niebuhr once observed, "that they embody the principle of resistance to government within the principle of government itself." [1]

Democracy does not mean merely that the majority

rules; in a far more fundamental sense it means that no majority has permanent power. Today's minority may become, by persuasion and voting, tomorrow's majority. A losing party accepts the verdict of an election because it is certain that there will be another day; the road to power in the future remains open to it on even legal terms. Under these circumstances it is wholly unnecessary for those who lose an election to erect barricades in the streets. This is why it is legitimate for a free society to forbid as criminal any attempt to change the going system by force, violence, or other illegal means.

It follows from all this that life in a political democracy is not an easy and comfortable one. From the psychic point of view, it is full of strain and friction. It offers little solace for those to whom relaxation is man's supreme achievement. It is not a congenial system for those who are convinced that we have already attained perfection, or at least as good a society as man can possibly hope to achieve, and that therefore the present moment in history should be frozen for all time to come. On the contrary, the atmosphere of a democratic society is one of perpetual strife; for the right to disagree includes of necessity the right to be disagreeable, to bicker, and to be contentious. In a democratic state the hue and cry of partisan political talk blankets the population like a Los Angeles smog. Where men are free, they are free to view with alarm as well as to point with pride. The prophets of doom are as free to speak their minds as the congenital optimists, the haters as well as the men of good will. When men are free and have a desire to learn, Milton once said, "there of necessity will be much arguing, much writing, many opinions." [2]

In short, a free society is inescapably a noisy and disorderly one, and this is hard on those who put an especially high premium on peace of mind and psychic security. It is also hard on the holders of public office, for they must stand up to the constant strain of criticism and opposition. A successful democratic politician needs a tough hide. It also takes a fairly tough hide to participate actively in the life of a functioning democracy as a citizen. Those who put a high price on mental peace and psychic security are disturbed by the never-ending din. But from the nature of things the din cannot be ended, for to silence it would involve the substitution of a remedy far worse than the disease. We believe that life in a noisy society is infinitely preferable to life in a quiet penitentiary. Nevertheless, it must be clear that democratic government is government the hard way. The citizen of a democracy is compelled to face the facts of life, the unpleasant as well as the pleasant. For him there is no escape from many overt manifestations of group tension. In contrast, dictatorship manages to suppress at least the outward signs of group conflict by forbidding or at least minimizing the verbalization of social differences and tensions.

In many ways, democratic government asks much of people. Since it relies upon persuasion and reason, it asks them to do some thinking, and particularly, to think a great deal about difficult public questions. Every educator knows how very painful thinking really is, both for himself and his students. It can hardly be denied that many people have found a considerable measure of satisfaction in dictatorship because it releases them from the irksome obligation of thinking.[3] Furthermore, democracy asks us to be tolerant even of those with whom we may be in sharpest disagreement. Since intolerance of dissident opinions is certainly as "natural" as tolerance, and in fact seems to require much less of an exertion of will, this too is asking a good deal of us. Democracy is incorrigibly skeptical and tends therefore to be unsatisfying for those who demand the security of a full set of the correct answers to all the questions which perplex the human race. Democracy is not so much concerned with correct answers as it is with a methodology for reaching essentially tentative decisions in a workaday world.

We have to recognize that the price we must pay for living in a free speech society is very great, though of course we are persuaded that the price is not too great.

We are apt to be the most acutely aware of the steepness of the price when men exercise the right to talk politics. Talk described as radical is usually, though of course not always, political talk. Most people know from their own experience that ideas can be dangerous, and ideas are couched in words. At best, political talk can be disturbing, merely because it is contentious; and at worst, where such talk strikes at the central values of our economic and governmental system, it can be very frightening indeed.

Yet we must be prepared to understand—if our system is to operate along the lines of its essential principles—that the right to speak freely must include the right to talk about things that matter most. The Justices of the Supreme Court, virtually without dissent, have long been committed to this proposition. A democratic system of government cannot avoid taking the risks of freedom, and full citizenship in such a system calls for a measure of self-confidence and civic courage. This is what Justice Brandeis had in mind when he wrote in a post-World War I case: "Those who won our independence by revolution were not cowards. They did not fear political change. They did not exalt order at the cost of liberty." [4] He said that "they valued liberty both as an end and as means. They believed liberty to be the secret of happiness and courage to be the secret of liberty. . . . They recognized the risks to which all human

institutions are subject. But they knew that order cannot be secured merely through fear of punishment for
its infraction; that it is hazardous to discourage thought,
hope and imagination; that fear breeds repression; that
repression breeds hate; that hate menaces stable government; that the path of safety lies in the opportunity to
discuss freely supposed grievances and proposed remedies; and that the fitting remedy for evil counsels is
good ones." [5]

There has been no dissonance in the views of most
Justices on this score. Thus Justice Black once wrote:
"We must have freedom of speech for all or we will in
the long run have it for none but the cringing and the
craven." [6] And more recently he stated: "The First
Amendment provides the only kind of security system
that can preserve a free government—one that leaves the
way wide open for people to favor, discuss, advocate, or
incite causes and doctrines however obnoxious and an-
tagonistic such views may be to the rest of us." [7] In the
oft-quoted words of Justice Holmes, "if there is any
principle of the Constitution that more imperatively
calls for attachment than any other it is the principle of
free thought—not free thought for those who agree with
us but freedom for the thought that we hate." [8]

Justice Jackson recorded some memorable words on
this subject in 1950 when he wrote: "While the Governments, State and Federal, have expansive powers to cur-

tail action, and some small powers to curtail speech or writing, I think neither has any power, on any pretext, directly or indirectly to attempt foreclosure of any line of thought. Our forefathers found the evils of free thinking more to be endured than the evils of inquest or suppression. . . . Intellectual freedom means the right to re-examine much that has been long taken for granted. A free man must be a reasoning man, and he must dare to doubt what a legislative or electoral majority may most passionately assert. The danger that citizens will think wrongly is serious, but less dangerous than atrophy from not thinking at all. Our Constitution relies on our electorate's complete ideological freedom to nourish independent and responsible intelligence and preserve our democracy from that submissiveness, timidity and herd-mindedness of the masses which would foster a tyranny of mediocrity. . . . It is not the function of our Government to keep the citizen from falling into error; it is the function of the citizen to keep the Government from falling into error." [9]

In a famous opinion holding that press censorship is not constitutionally justified merely because a newspaper publishes scurrilous attacks upon public officials and others, Chief Justice Hughes observed: "Charges of reprehensible conduct, and in particular of official malfeasance, unquestionably create a public scandal, but the theory of the constitutional guaranty is that even a more serious public evil would be caused by authority to prevent publication." [10] Similarly, in the Dennis case,[11] Chief Justice Vinson carefully pointed out that in adopting the Smith Act, "Congress did not intend to eradicate the free discussion of political theories, to destroy the traditional rights of Americans to discuss and evaluate ideas without fear of governmental sanction." And though Justice Frankfurter concurred with the judgment of the Court, he filed a lengthy and brilliantly incisive opinion, in which he asserted: "The history of civilization is in considerable measure the displacement of error which once held sway as official truth by beliefs which in turn have yielded to other truths. Therefore the liberty of man to search for truth ought not to be fettered, no matter what orthodoxies he may challenge. Liberty of thought soon shrivels without freedom of expression. Nor can truth be pursued in an atmosphere hostile to the endeavor or under dangers which are hazarded only by heroes." [12]

As Judge Learned Hand once pointed out, the First Amendment "presupposes that there are no orthodoxies —religious, political, economic, or scientific—which are immune from debate and dispute. Back of that is the assumption—itself an orthodoxy, and the one permissible exception—that truth will be most likely to emerge, if no limitations are imposed upon utterances that can with any plausibility be regarded as efforts to present grounds for accepting or rejecting propositions whose truth the utterer asserts, or denies." [13]

2

It cannot be denied that freedom of speech has been under severe pressure at various times in the course of American history. The Founding Fathers who wrote and ratified the First Amendment were well aware of the numerous English and colonial prosecutions for common law sedition, and particularly seditious libel—among which John Peter Zenger's case had been a true *cause célèbre* [14]—and they fully intended, as Chafee has put it, "to wipe out the common law of sedition, and make further prosecutions for criticism of the government, without any incitement to law-breaking, forever impossible in the United States of America." [15] During the early years of the Republic, when war with France and/or England hung in the balance, the Alien and Sedition Acts of 1798, adopted by a frightened Federalist government, imposed drastic limitations on free speech, and the history of their enforcement is a sorry story indeed.[16] Some of the provisions in this legislation seem to us almost incredible. The Sedition Act of 1798 actually made it a crime to "write . . . or publish . . . any false, scandalous and malicious writing . . . against the government of the United States, or either house of the Congress of the United States, or the President of the United States, with intent to defame . . ." them "or to excite against them, . . . the hatred of the good people of the United States, . . ." [17]

In the three decades before the Civil War, there was a great deal of mob activity which interfered with the free exercise of the right to talk politics, and especially with the speech rights of the abolitionists. William Lloyd Garrison was mobbed in Boston, and the religious publisher, Elijah P. Lovejoy, was murdered in Alton, Illinois.[18] During the great crisis of the Civil War itself many thousands of people were arrested and held without charge in military prisons for having expressed opinions regarded as disloyal, and President Lincoln stoutly defended his suspension of habeas corpus without statutory permission as necessary to save the union.[19]

Perhaps the worst period of our history, insofar as the exercise of the right of free speech is concerned, came during and immediately after World War I, particularly under the far-reaching authority of the Espionage Act of 1917 and the Sedition Act of 1918.[20] Under these statutes, which were administered in a very excited public atmosphere, a great many things happened of which we are now, upon mature reflection, thoroughly ashamed. Men received lengthy jail sentences, for example, for arguing that the war should be financed through heavier taxation rather than through the sale of bonds. Men were punished for refusing to contribute to the Y.M.C.A. The Palmer raids, in January, 1920, directed against aliens suspected of political radicalism, were aptly described by a high governmental official of that day as "deportation delirium." [21] The ousting of the five duly elected Socialist members of the New York Assembly in January, 1920, which Charles Evans Hughes criticized so powerfully,[22] and the expulsion of the Socialist Victor L. Berger from the federal House of Representatives in 1919, were dramatic parts of this story.[23] In many ways, the celebrated Sacco-Vanzetti case was the final and perhaps inevitable fruit of the post-World War I hysteria.[24]

From the point of view of the freedom of political expression, the record during World War II was quite free from the excesses of World War I, partly, perhaps, because the earlier record had been so very bad.[25] But in the aftermath of this great war there was another period of hysteria which ran its fitful course and ultimately fizzled out under the hot but revealing klieg lights of television.

But however much the right to talk politics has on

occasion been invaded by community pressures in times of crisis, American courts, and particularly the United States Supreme Court, have on the whole maintained a generous construction of the liberty of speech. Of course, exceptional circumstances have been recognized where the right to speak yields in some measure to a counter-vailing interest. Perhaps the best-known example is the Court's holding that the right to talk politics may be limited by the government in the case of civil servants in the classified service.[26] The Court sustained the con-stitutionality of Section 9 of the Hatch Act of 1940,[27] which forbids employees in the executive branch of the government, with certain exceptions at policy-making levels, from taking "any active part in political manage-ment or in political campaigns." It argued that, as in other cases, it must balance the extent of the guaranties of freedom from Congressional enactments designed to protect a democratic society against the supposed evil of political partisanship by classified employees of the government. If Congress believes that efficiency in the public service may be best obtained by prohibiting ac-tive participation by classified employees in politics, the Court could see no constitutional objection, since this was an allowable and reasonable judgment.

In the leading case dealing with the validity of the federal loyalty-security program as applied to civil serv-ants, the Court of Appeals for the District of Columbia brushed aside objections based on the First Amendment, taking the position that the Constitution does not forbid the dismissal of government employees because of their political beliefs, activities or affiliations.[28] Judge Prettyman made the familiar point that "the First Amendment guarantees free speech and assembly, but it does not guarantee Government employ." [29] Although the Supreme Court affirmed this judgment, it did so by a 4 to 4 division, and thus no opinions were filed.[30] Later Supreme Court decisions dealing with aspects of the federal fidelity program have all managed to avoid constitutional issues by focusing on tangential statutory questions.[31] Loyalty programs for state officials [32] and local school teachers [33] have also been upheld against various constitutional objections. Speaking of school teachers, Justice Minton said that it was clear that persons have the right "to assemble, speak, think and believe as they will," but that "it is equally clear that they have no right to work for the State in the school system on their own terms. . . . They may work for the school system upon the reasonable terms laid down by the proper authorities. . . . If they do not choose to work on such terms, they are at liberty to retain their beliefs and associations and go elsewhere." [34] It should be noted that Justice Black dissented, protesting against "rapidly multiplying legislative enactments which make it dangerous—this time for school teachers—

to think or say anything except what a transient majority happen to approve at the moment." [35] Justice Douglas also dissented, arguing that he could not accept the doctrine that government employees are second class citizens who must sacrifice their civil rights.

Another well-known illustration of a decision in which the Court subordinated an unfettered right to talk politics to a compelling social interest was the case [36] which upheld the non-Communist affidavit section (Section 9h) of the Taft-Hartley Act of 1947. [37] The statute denies access to the facilities of the National Labor Relations Board to any union whose officers have not filed an affidavit that they are not members of the Communist party. The Court found that the purpose of the act was to eliminate the obstruction to interstate commerce which results from political strikes, and that substantial evidence had been submitted to Congress showing that Communist leaders of labor unions had in the past and would in the future subordinate legitimate trade union objectives to obstructive strikes when dictated by party leaders, often in support of a foreign government. The Court pointed out that if constitutional government is to survive—and First Amendment freedoms depend upon such survival—then it must have the power to protect itself against unlawful conduct. Freedom of speech, said Chief Justice Vinson, "does not comprehend the right to speak on any subject at any time."

In fact, the Court insisted that the statute in question did not really affect speech, but only a form of harmful conduct which Congress has determined is carried on by persons who may be identified by their political affiliations and beliefs. The statute is designed to protect the public, not against what Communists advocate or believe, but against what Congress has concluded they have done and are likely to do again. In any event, the Court found that the effect of the statute upon First Amendment freedoms was "relatively small" and that, in contrast, the public interest to be protected was substantial. It noted that it had often recognized that the public has a right to be protected from evils of conduct, citing as examples cases dealing with sound trucks, unauthorized parades, child labor, public health or morals, civil servants, and members of the bar.

Nevertheless, it is still true that freedom to talk politics is the rule, and that the restraint is at best an exception which requires special justification. Even in treason cases the Supreme Court was careful, during World War II, to hold the government to very strict standards of proof.[38] In a leading case brought under the Espionage Act, the Court ruled that the government had to prove beyond a reasonable doubt that the defendant had published certain articles attacking the war effort with the specific intent or evil purpose of accomplishing the purpose which is punished by the statute.[39] During the period between the two world wars, the Court made several important decisions dealing with the range of the right to talk politics. It held that prior censorship was constitutionally inadmissible even in the case of a scandal-mongering weekly newspaper which specialized in making scurrilous attacks upon public officials.[40] It also ruled that speech at a public meeting which is otherwise lawful cannot be punished by the state merely because the meeting was held under the auspices of the Communist party.[41] Chief Justice Hughes affirmed that "peaceable assembly for lawful discussion cannot be made a crime. The holding of meetings for peaceable political action cannot be proscribed. . . . The question, if the rights of free speech and peaceable assembly are to be preserved, is not as to the auspices under which the meeting is held but as to its purpose; not as to the relations of the speakers, but whether their utterances transcend the bounds of the freedom of speech which the Constitution protects." [42] In 1927, the Court held unconstitutional a Kansas statute which, as construed by the state's highest court, made it a crime to join an organization which teaches that the "class struggle" is inevitable.[43] The absence of evidence that the organization advocated any crime, violence, or other unlawful acts or methods as a means of effecting industrial or political changes was regarded as decisive. In 1931, the Court set aside a conviction under a California "red flag" law on the ground that it punished the opportunity for free political discussion.[44] As Justice Roberts asserted in the well-known Herndon case,[45] the power of the state to restrict freedom of speech "must find its justification in a reasonable apprehension of danger to organized government. The judgment of the legislature is not unfettered. The limitation upon individual liberty must have appropriate relation to the safety of the state."

During World War II the Court ruled, in the Schneiderman case,[46] that in a denaturalization proceeding, where the government must present evidence of "a clear and convincing character," it must not be presumed that Congress intended to circumscribe the liberty of political thought when it adopted the general phrases of the denationalization statute, and that all doubts must be resolved in favor of the retention of citizenship. The Court also decided that the right to speak to people about trade unionism was protected by the guaranty of free speech, and that in the setting of a lawful and orderly assembly there was no such danger to public welfare as to justify limiting the freedom of a trade union official to solicit new members.[47] Accordingly, it held

that a state may not lawfully require a trade union official to register with a public official in order to make a
public speech.

Several years later, the Court avoided ruling on the
constitutionality of Section 304 of the Taft-Hartley
Act—which made unlawful any trade union expenditure
or contribution in connection with any federal election
—by holding, in the case of a union which published
political statements in its weekly newspaper, that Congress did not intend to reach a house organ publishing
political news in the regular course of its operations.[48]
Speaking in behalf of four concurring Justices who
wanted to hold the act invalid, Justice Rutledge said:
"The expression of bloc sentiment is and always has
been an integral part of our democratic electoral and
legislative processes. They could hardly go on without
it." [49]

3

I doubt very much whether we have ever had a Justice
on the Supreme Court bench who did not recognize the
primacy of the right to talk politics freely for our democratic society. Nor, on the other hand, have we ever had

a Justice who felt that there are no possible legitimate limits to such speech. The problem has been to find a formula or a rationale to define as precisely as possible the nature of these limits. And it is clear from the voluminous record on this subject that there has never been agreement on the formula. I think that many variations among the formulations of the Justices have been elaborated at a mere verbal level, and that what has probably counted most has been the judge's reaction to and interpretation of the concrete fact situation presented in the case. I suggest that the judicial feel for a situation has been more significant than the words employed to translate it into an opinion. Thus in the Dennis case,[50] of the eight Justices participating, six had the feeling that Congress had not acted unreasonably in believing that what the eleven Communist leaders had said and done was sufficiently dangerous to the state to warrant the imposition of criminal penalties. The two dissenters drew from the same facts the inference that there had been no clear and present danger to the state sufficiently acute and urgent to justify the restriction on speech.

Although much has been said about the "clear and present danger" test which Justices Holmes and Brandeis elaborated in the ten-year period following World War I, it is very doubtful whether a majority of the Justices, at any given time, have been willing to accept it as the touchstone of decision.[51] It will be recalled that in a series of cases beginning in the spring of 1919 [52] Justices Holmes and Brandeis argued that speech may not be proscribed unless it has created a clear and present danger of a serious evil that the legislature has a right to prevent. Punishment is constitutionally legitimate, Justice Brandeis maintained, only if "the incidence of the evil apprehended is so imminent that it may befall before there is opportunity for full discussion. If there be time to expose through discussion the falsehood and fallacies, to avert the evil by the processes of education, the remedy to be applied is more speech, not enforced silence. Only an emergency can justify repression. Such must be the rule if authority can justify repression." [53]

But it is worth noting that Holmes and Brandeis never used the clear and present danger doctrine as the test of the validity of legislation. In the six wartime free speech cases arising under the Espionage Act of 1917 in which they voted, whether they stood with the majority [54] or voted against sustaining convictions on the ground that the clear and present danger test had not been met,[55] they never questioned the constitutionality of the statute itself. They were concerned, not with the statute, but with an assessment of the nature and consequences of the speech in question. What they tried to develop was a sort of rule of reason which might serve as an administrative standard to guide those who are concerned with handling actual cases.[56] They tried to give sympathetic prosecutors, judges, and juries a working principle which in concrete situations would militate in favor of allowing speech the widest possible latitude.

Other Justices, however, soon developed a basic variation of the Holmes–Brandeis danger doctrine. First elaborated by Justice Sanford in 1925, in the Gitlow case,[57] where a conviction under the New York criminal anarchy law was sustained, this view was that where the lawmaking body itself declares in effect that the use of certain words under certain conditions creates a clear and present danger of a serious evil, then, unless the legislative judgment is clearly unreasonable and without foundation, the only question to be decided in a case arising under such a statute is whether the defendant actually used the proscribed words.

Gitlow's prosecution was based on the fact that he had published a "Left Wing Manifesto" advocating proletarian revolution. There was, of course, no evidence that the publication had any effect at all. Of this silly pamphlet Professor Chafee once said: "Any agitator who read these thirty-four pages to a mob would not stir them to violence, except possibly against himself. This Manifesto would disperse them faster than the Riot Act. It is best described by recalling the Mouse in *Alice in*

Wonderland reading about the Norman Conquest to dry off the Dodo and the Lory. 'Ahem,' said the Mouse with an important air, 'are you all ready? This is the driest thing I know.' " [58] Without saying anything about the validity of the statute, Justices Holmes and Brandeis dissented, arguing that Gitlow's publication had not in fact posed a clear and present danger.

It was the Gitlow version of the clear and present danger doctrine which Judge Medina applied in the Smith Act prosecutions of the top Communist leaders in 1949, and which Chief Justice Vinson accepted for the Court when the case came up on appeal.[59] The Smith Act, enacted in 1940, makes it unlawful, "knowingly or wilfully" to "advocate, abet, advise, or teach the duty, necessity, desirability, or propriety of overthrowing or destroying any government in the United States by force or violence," or to publish printed matter having this purpose, or to organize a group having this purpose. In his charge to the jury, Judge Medina said he found "as matter of law that there is sufficient danger of substantive evil that the Congress has a right to prevent to justify the application of the statute under the First Amendment of the Constitution. This is a matter of law about which you have no concern." [60]

This interpretation was approved by Judge Learned Hand when he spoke for the Second Court of Appeals in affirming the conviction.[61] He held that it was only proper for the jury to decide whether the defendants had violated the statute; for, he asserted, "whether the mischief of the repression is greater than the gravity of the evil, discounted by its improbability," was not a question of fact at all. "Were it not so," he added, "there would be no chance for review, for the verdict would be final; moreover, different juries might give different verdicts, and any approach to uniformity . . . would be impossible." [62] Speaking for the Supreme Court, Chief Justice Vinson agreed that the question as to whether the statute was directed against a substantive evil which posed a clear and present danger Congress had the power to punish was not a jury question, but only a question of law, because it involved an interpretation of the scope of the First Amendment.

Not only have Justices of the Supreme Court held to different versions of the clear and present danger doctrine, but some have ignored it altogether, including such stout champions of civil liberty as Chief Justices Hughes [63] and Stone.[64] Still others, notably Justice Frankfurter, himself strongly committed to the philosophy of civil liberty, have actually rejected the danger doctrine. He once asserted that Justice Holmes never used his concept "to express a technical legal doctrine or to convey a formula for adjudicating cases," but rather that it was "a literary phrase not to be distorted by being taken from its context." [65] He objected to the use of the clear and present danger standard in the flag salute case, declaring that its application as a measure of permissible educational policy was "to take a felicitous phrase out of the context of the particular situation where it arose and for which it was adapted." [66] Justice Jackson thought that the clear and present danger test was all right for its time, but that it was unsuited for an era which has revealed "the subtlety and efficacy of modernized revolutionary techniques used by totalitarian parties." [67] He said that "when the issue is criminality of a hot-headed speech on a street corner, or circulation of a few incendiary pamphlets, or parading by some zealots behind a red flag, or refusal of a handful of school children to salute our flag, it is not beyond the capacity of the judicial process to gather, comprehend and weigh the necessary materials for decision whether it is a clear and present danger of substantive evil or a harmless letting off of steam." [68] But when the problem is that of a well-organized, nation-wide conspiracy, Justice Jackson argued, the clear and present danger doctrine would hold the government "captive in a judge-made verbal trap." In dealing with the Communist conspiracy in the context of contemporary conditions, he insisted that Congress was in a better position than the courts to appraise the imponderables, including both national and international phenomena, which have a bearing upon any assessment of the magnitude and urgency of the problem.

Many scholars have criticized the clear and present danger rule from various points of view. Alexander Meiklejohn, for example, objected that the doctrine establishes the right of legislative control more than it defends the right of free speech, arguing that it justified the suppression of dissident minorities in "dangerous" times and exalted majority decisions over constitutional right.[69] Others have expressed opposition to the doctrine on the ground that it is a subjective test with which only men like Holmes and Brandeis can be trusted, and that it is too vague and uncertain to be a reliable guide to decision. Still others have taken the position that the rule opens the door too wide for subversive activity inimical to the security of the state.[70] In the light of the wide differences of opinion which judges have had about the doctrine, there is much substance to the observation of an astute constitutional law scholar that "if by law we mean a reasonably accurate prediction as to how a court will dispose of a given controversy, the clear and present danger test has never been law." [71]

What test, then, does prevail in the courts? I suggest that whatever the verbal formulation has been, the test is essentially a rule of reason. None of the judges who have most explicitly rejected the clear and present danger test has ever suggested that in spelling out restraints upon speech the legislative body may do as it pleases. I can think of no Supreme Court Justice who has ever expressed a willingness to surrender his power of judicial review, that is to say, the power to rule on the constitutionality of statutes. Not even Justice Frankfurter, who is the present Court's leading spokesman for the doctrine of judicial self-restraint, will go that far. Many Justices, as I have indicated, including men strongly committed to the maximum protection of civil liberties, have ruled on the reasonableness of legislation affecting speech without paying any attention to the clear and present danger test. Whether the judge travels one road or another, the question always seems to be: Did the law-making body, in imposing the restraint, act reasonably, in the light of all relevant facts and circumstances? In the alternative, the question for an appellate court is: Assuming the validity of the statute, was its application in the concrete case reasonable in the light of all the facts and circumstances? For a constitutional statute may be applied in an unconstitutional way.

Of course, any rule of reason is necessarily vague. It is equally vague in the anti-trust field, but without such a rule the Sherman Act would be invalid.[72] There are a great many vaguely formulated doctrines in the law, since not all doctrines can be stated in precise terms. But just as natural law is the essential underpinning of a humane society,[73] so is the principle of reasonableness necessary for a truly constitutional system of government. And although it is manifestly impossible to define reasonableness in the abstract with any precision, it ought to be comforting to know that after a legislature has adopted a law, perhaps under the influence of great emotion, and then pursuant to the statute a court has convicted a man, perhaps a member of a marginal social group, an appeal still lies to an independent bench of judges who enjoy life tenure and who are completely insulated against the hazards of political retribution. That the Justices are also human need not be argued, of course, but it should be remembered that they are deeply conditioned by membership in a great and honorable institution which has its own time-tested methods, traditions, and commitments to constitutional principles. To a considerable extent, judgment is based on a record, the issues are explored through argument of opposing counsel, and the facts of life as well as the lessons of history are examined to arrive at a decision. The rationale supporting the decision is then written out in an opinion which, by its very nature, is a product of reason and an appeal to reason. The opinion is printed for all to read, and to appraise or criticize as they please, and the Justices profit greatly from the criticism.

One should not minimize the fact that in our separation of powers system, one who has been convicted of violating an arbitrary statute, or of an arbitrary application of a statute, has still another chance to get the issue of arbitrariness tested in a great tribunal which is as disinterested as human institutions are ever likely to be. It is gross exaggeration to say that this means that the Supreme Court rules the nation, since most questions of life are not litigable questions at all, and in any event, most legal questions do not get settled there. Furthermore, at the very most all the Court has is a veto power; the initiative in government lies elsewhere.

Finally, many judges make it perfectly clear that in the free speech cases they seek to measure the relative weight of the various factors of the situation. I suspect that most judges, even including those who do not say as much, do just that. Judgment in specific cases turns on a number of questions. How serious is the danger created by the speech? How imminent is the danger? How much interference with speech will result from a holding against the speaker? Is there some less drastic way of dealing with the danger? What was the intent of the speaker? Will more speech suffice to handle this one? Is the price of restraint too great, in the light of the magnitude of the evil at hand? As Professor Freund once observed, "No matter how rapidly we utter the phrase 'clear and present danger,' or how closely we hyphenate the words, they are not a substitute for the weighing of values. They tend to convey a delusion of certitude when what is most certain is the complexity of the strands in the web of freedoms which the judge must disentangle." [74] Judge Learned Hand expressed this thought very clearly in his review of the Dennis case for the Court of Appeals, when he asserted, "no longer can there be any doubt, if indeed there was before, that the phrase, 'clear and present danger,' is not a slogan or a shibboleth to be applied as though it carried its own meaning; but that it involves in every case a comparison between interests which are to be appraised qualitatively." [75] Justice Frankfurter may have used hyperbole when he referred to the clear and present danger doctrine as "a sonorous formula which is in fact only a euphemistic disguise for an unresolved conflict"; but one cannot quarrel with his further statement that "if adjudication is to be a rational process, we cannot escape a candid examination of the conflicting claims with full recognition that both are supported by weighty title-deeds." [76]

4

Attention should be drawn to one final distinction made in the law, dealing with the limits of the right to talk politics. It is the distinction between advocacy or agitation, which is not constitutionally punishable, and direct incitement of unlawful action, which is punishable. It is now perfectly clear that this distinction is made by most American judges, and it has been asserted over and over again by the Supreme Court. It is one of our principal legal guaranties of a wide latitude of political free speech.

During World War I, in a case involving a radical magazine, *The Masses,* Judge Learned Hand spelled out the nature of the distinction between legitimate and illegitimate advocacy.[77] He wrote:

One may not counsel or advise others to violate the law as it stands. Words are not only the keys of persuasion, but the triggers of action, and those which have no purport but to counsel the violation of law cannot by any latitude of interpretation be a part of that public opinion which is the final source of government in a democratic state. . . . Political agitation, by the passions it arouses or the convictions it engenders, may in fact stimulate men to the violation of law. Detestation of existing policies is easily transformed into forcible resistance of the authority which puts them in execution, and it would be folly to disregard the causal relation between the two. Yet to assimilate agitation, legitimate as such, with direct incitement to violent resistance, is to disregard the tolerance of all methods of political agitation which in normal times is a safeguard of free government. The distinction is not a scholastic subterfuge, but a hard-bought acquisition in the fight for freedom, and the purpose to disregard it must be evident when the power exists. If one stops short of urging upon others that it is their duty or their interest to resist the law, it seems to me one should not be held to have attempted to cause its violation.

The Supreme Court asserted in June, 1957, that "the distinction between advocacy of abstract doctrine and advocacy directed at promoting unlawful action is one that has been consistently recognized" by it since World War I.[78] For example, in the Gitlow case, decided in 1925, Justice Sanford was careful to note of the statute before it, the New York Criminal Anarchy Act, that it "does not penalize the utterance or publication of abstract 'doctrine' or academic discussion having no quality of incitement to any concrete action. It is not aimed against mere historical or philosophical essays. It does not restrain the advocacy of changes in the form of government by constitutional and lawful means. What it prohibits is language advocating, advising, or teaching the overthrow of organized government by unlawful means. These words imply urging to action. . . . It is not the abstract 'doctrine' of overthrowing organized government by unlawful means which is denounced by the statute, but the advocacy of action for the accomplishment of that purpose." [79]

The most important federal statute of our times which sets limits upon free speech is the Smith Act of

1940. In the prosecutions brought under this statute, federal judges have been careful to make the distinction between advocacy of ideas and incitement of unlawful action. In his famous charge to the jury in the Dennis prosecutions, Judge Medina declared "that it is not the abstract doctrine of overthrowing or destroying organized government by unlawful means which is denounced by this law, but the teaching and advocacy of action for the accomplishment of that purpose, by language reasonably and ordinarily calculated to incite persons to such action, . . . as speedily as circumstances would permit." [80] In upholding the Dennis convictions, Chief Justice Vinson, who delivered the opinion of the Court, spoke approvingly of the trial judge's distinction between advocacy of action and the discussion of ideas, and carefully noted that "Congress did not intend to eradicate the free discussion of political theories, to destroy the traditional rights of Americans to discuss and evaluate ideas without fear of governmental sanction." [81] In his separate concurring opinion, Justice Frankfurter noted that "throughout our decisions there has recurred a distinction between the statement of an idea which may prompt its hearers to take unlawful action, and advocacy that such action be taken." [82] While he conceded that there was no divining rod by which "advocacy" might be located, and that the "exposition of ideas readily merges into advocacy," Justice Frankfurter added: "But there is underlying validity in the distinction between advocacy and the interchange of ideas, and we do not discard a useful tool because it may be misused." [83] Similarly, Justice Jackson said, in his concurring opinion: "Of course, it is not always easy to distinguish teaching or advocacy in the sense of incitement from teaching or advocacy in the sense of exposition or explanation. It is a question of fact in each case." [84]

How much importance the Supreme Court attaches to this distinction was illustrated by its much-discussed decision in the Yates case,[85] decided in 1957. This case involved the appeals of a number of second-string Communist leaders who had been convicted in the Southern California federal district court of violating the Smith Act. On the charge of advocating the unlawful overthrow of government, the trial judge had refused to instruct the jury (as he had been requested by both sides) that the statute does not forbid mere advocacy of abstract doctrine, but only incitement to action to accomplish the proscribed end. The Court held, Justice Clark dissenting alone, that this was reversible error. Speaking for the majority, Justice Harlan argued that the Court should not assume "that Congress chose to disregard a constitutional danger zone so clearly marked" as that which is implicit in the distinction between advocacy of ideas and incitement to action. Indeed he was sure, from a study of legislative history, that Congress was fully aware of the distinction and did not intend to disregard it. Thus the trial judge was wrong in telling the jury that advocacy was punishable whether in the language of incitement or not. "The essential distinction," said Justice Harlan, "is that those to whom the advocacy is addressed must be urged to *do* something, now or in the future, rather than merely to *believe* in something." [86] He added that the spelling out of this distinction went to the very heart of the charges against the defendants.

5

The right to talk politics is indispensable for the proper functioning of a free society. Since democracy would be a snare and a delusion without this right, it holds a preferred position in our political theory and constitutional law. Like all rights, it is not absolute, and incitement to unlawful action may properly be punished by the state. Democracy has no obligation of any kind to commit suicide. But short of the point of incitement to crime, our system must rely upon the free flow of ideas. Far more wonderful than our oversized automobiles, our television and air-conditioning, our jet planes and our hydrogen bombs, is the free human mind. Good government, the cultivation of the arts, the progress of the sciences and technology, all require an atmosphere of freedom of thought and of freedom to put thoughts into words. The price may seem to be a steep one, but what is purchased is the greatest bargain in all history.

Notes

Religious Freedom in America—More or Less

1 See Joseph L. Blau, *Cornerstones of Religious Freedom in America* (Boston: Beacon Press, 1949); Anson Phelps Stokes, *Church and State in the United States* (3 vols., New York: Harper, 1950).

2 James Bryce, *The American Commonwealth* (rev. ed., New York: Macmillan, 1913), II, 763.

3 Phillips Bradley, ed., *Democracy in America* (New York: Knopf, 1948), I, 308.

4 Bryce, II, 766.

5 New York Constitution, Art. I, §3. Many state constitutions have similar qualifying phrases. See, e.g., the Colorado Constitution, Art. II, §4: ". . . but, the liberty of conscience hereby secured shall not be construed to dispense with oaths or affirmations, excuse acts of licentiousness, or justify practices inconsistent with the good order, peace or safety of the state."

6 H. T. Dohrman, *California Cult* (Boston: Beacon Press, 1958), p. ix. This is an engrossing analysis of the "Mankind United" cult. See also Elmer Talmage Clark, *The Small Sects in America* (rev. ed., Nashville: Abingdon-Cokesbury Press, 1949); Charles S. Braden, *These Also Believe* (New York: Macmillan, 1949); Stokes, III, 548–550.

7 Bradley, ed., *Democracy in America,* II, 134.

8 *United States* v. *Ballard,* 322 U.S. 78 (1944). For an account of the "I Am" movement, see Braden, Chap. 7.

9 Transcript, p. 129.

10 Transcript, pp. 594–595.

11 Transcript, p. 746.

12 Transcript, p. 775.

13 Transcript, p. 158.

14 Brief for the Ballards, *United States* v. *Ballard,* 322 U.S. 78 (1944), p. 101.

15 Transcript, p. 1496.

16 *Ballard* v. *United States,* 138 F.2d 540 (9th Cir. 1943).

17 Brief for the Ballards, p. 32.

18 *Ibid.,* pp. 41–42.

19 322 U.S. 86–87. For earlier mail fraud cases, where only the question of good faith was allowed to go to the jury, see *United States* v. *White,* 150 Fed. 379 (D. Md. 1906); *Post* v. *United States,* 135 Fed. 1 (5th Cir. 1905); *New* v. *United States,* 245 Fed. 710 (9th Cir. 1917), *cert. denied,* 246 U.S. 665 (1918).

20 322 U.S. 87.

21 *Id.*

22 *Id.*

23 322 U.S. 88–89.

24 322 U.S. 92.

25 322 U.S. 94.

26 *Id.*

27 322 U.S. 95.

28 *Archives of Maryland,* I, 246.

29 *Archives of Maryland,* I, 245.

30 For the texts, see Blau, pp. 74–87.

31 *Illinois* ex rel. *McCollum* v. *Board of Education,* 333 U.S. 203, 211 (1948).

32 The New York legislature enacted a statute on April 20, 1784, disestablishing the Episcopal Church, declaring that colonial laws compelling the payment of taxes for its support were "contrary to every principle of justice and sound policy." N.Y. Laws, 7th Sess., 1784, c. 38.

33 *Basic Writings of Thomas Paine* (New York: Willey Book Co., 1942), p. 52.

34 J. Welch, in *Board of Education of Cincinnati* v. *Minor*, 23 Ohio St. 211, 248 (1872).

35 See Don J. Hager, "Introduction: Religious Conflict," *The Journal of Social Issues*, XII, No. 3 (1956), 3: "In 1955 it was reported that 97 million Americans claim affiliation with some place of worship and that they contributed at least $2,000,000,000 to the support of church and synagogue. Over one-half billion dollars were invested in the construction of new church buildings and schools. It is claimed that Sunday school registration is at an all-time high. The statistics used to record the growth of religious organizations in the United States are not, of course, beyond debate and criticism; but they do sustain the popular image of church and synagogue as thriving and vigorous institutional structures." See also *Yearbook of American Churches* (1958), p. iv, which reports that 62 per cent of the population claim membership in some religious organization.

36 Claud D. Nelson, *Church and State* (New York: National Council of the Churches of Christ in the United States of America, 1953), p. 1. See also Loren P. Beth, "Toward a Modern American Theory of Church-State Relationships," *Political Science Quarterly*, LXX (December, 1955), 573–597.

37 *Watson* v. *Jones*, 13 Wall. (U.S.) 679 (1871); *Kedroff* v. *St. Nicholas Cathedral*, 344 U.S. 94 (1952).

38 *Reynolds* v. *United States*, 98 U.S. 145, 164 (1878).

39 *Davis* v. *Beason*, 133 U.S. 333, 342 (1890). This case upheld a territorial statute forbidding polygamists to vote. See also *Mormon Church* v. *United States*, 136 U.S. 1 (1890); *State* v. *Barlow*, 107 Utah 292, 153 P.2d 647 (1944), *appeal dismissed for want of a substantial federal question*, 324 U.S. 829 (1945).

40 321 U.S. 158 (1944).

41 Clement E. Vose, "Litigation as a Form of Pressure Group Activity," *Annals of the American Academy*, Vol. 319 (September, 1958), 20–31, 22. See especially *Cantwell* v. *Connecticut*, 310 U.S. 296 (1940); *West Virginia State Board of Education* v. *Barnette*, 319 U.S. 624 (1943); *Murdock* v. *Pennsylvania*, 319 U.S. 105 (1943).

42 *Prince* v. *Massachusetts*, 321 U.S. at 166.

43 *Ibid.*, at 170.

44 The leading English decision was *Regina* v. *Senior*, 1 Q.B. Div. 283 (1899). The leading Canadian case was *Rex* v. *Lewis*, 6 Ont. L. Rep. 132

(1903). See C. C. Cawley, "Criminal Liability in Faith Healing," *Minnesota Law Review*, XXXIX (December, 1954), 48–74.

45   The leading decision was *People* v. *Pierson*, 176 N.Y. 201, 68 N.E. 243 (1903).

46   *People* ex rel. *Wallace* v. *Labrenz*, 411 Ill. 618, 104 N.E.2d 769 (1952), *cert. denied*, 344 U.S. 824 (1952); *Mitchell* v. *Davis*, 205 S.W.2d 812 (Tex. Civ. App. 1947); *Morrison* v. *State*, 252 S.W.2d 97 (Mo. App. 1952). *Contra: In re Hudson*, 13 Wash. 2d 673, 126 P.2d 765 (1942).

47   See *State* v. *Verbon*, 167 Wash. 140, 8 P.2d 1083 (1932); *Smith* v. *People*, 51 Colo. 270, 117 P. 612 (1911); *People* v. *Handzik*, 410 Ill. 295, 102 N.E.2d 340 (1951), *cert. denied*, 343 U.S. 927 (1951). Consult: Beverly Lake, "Freedom to Worship Curiously," *University of Florida Law Review*, I (Summer, 1948), 203–241.

48   *Fealy* v. *City of Birmingham*, 15 Ala. App. 367, 372–373, 73 So. 296, 299 (1916).

49   *McMasters* v. *State*, 21 Okla. Cr. 318, 325, 207 P. 566, 569 (1922).

50   *Jacobson* v. *Massachusetts*, 197 U.S. 11 (1905).

51   See *Sadlock* v. *Board of Education*, 137 N.J.L. 85, 58 A.2d 218 (1948); *Mosier* v. *Barren County Board of Health*, 308 Ky. 829, 215 S.W.2d 967 (1948); *State* v. *Drew*, 89 N.H. 54, 192 A. 629 (1937).

52   *State* ex rel. *Holcomb* v. *Armstrong*, 39 Wash. 2d 860, 239 P.2d 545 (1952).

53   *Baer* v. *City of Bend*, 206 Ore. 221, 292 P.2d 134 (1956); *Dowell* v. *City of Tulsa, Okla.*, 273 P.2d 859, 43 A.L.R.2d 445 (Okla., 1954), *cert. denied*, 348 U.S. 912 (1955); *Kraus* v. *City of Cleveland*, 116 N.E.2d 779 (Com. Pl. Ohio 1953), 163 Ohio St. 559, 127 N.E.2d 609 (1955), *appeal dismissed for want of a substantial federal question*, 351 U.S. 935 (1956). See Donald R. McNeil, *The Fight for Fluoridation* (New York: Oxford, 1957).

54   *State* v. *Massey*, 229 N.C. 734, 51 S.E.2d 179 (1949), *appeal dismissed for want of a substantial federal question*, 336 U.S. 942 (1949); *Harden* v. *State*, 188 Tenn. 17, 216 S.W.2d 708 (1949). See John A. Womeldorf, "Rattlesnake Religion," *The Christian Century*, LXIV (December 10, 1947), 1517–1518.

55   *Lawson* v. *Commonwealth*, 291 Ky. 437, 164 S.W.2d 972 (1942); *Kirk* v. *Commonwealth*, 186 Va. 839, 44 S.E.2d. 409 (1947).

56   *State* v. *Massey, supra*, note 54.

57   *Davis* v. *Beason*, 133 U.S. 333, 342 (1890).

58 *In re Frazee,* 63 Mich. 396, 405–6, 30 N.W. 72, 75 (1886).

59 *Cleveland* v. *United States,* 329 U.S. 14, 20 (1946).

60 *Hamilton* v. *City of Montrose,* 109 Colo. 228, 124 P.2d 757 (1942); *Mashburn* v. *City of Bloomington,* 32 Ill. App. 245 (1889); *Commonwealth* v. *Plaisted,* 148 Mass. 375, 19 N.E. 224 (1889); *State* v. *White,* 64 N.H. 48, 5 Atl. 828 (1886). Even serious disturbances within a church building may be enjoined. *Morrison* v. *Rawlinson,* 193 S.C. 25, 7 S.E.2d 635 (1940).

61 *Chaplinsky* v. *New Hampshire,* 315 U.S. 568 (1942).

62 *Ibid.,* p. 572.

63 *Delk* v. *Commonwealth,* 166 Ky. 39, 47, 178 S.W. 1129, 1132 (1915).

64 *People* v. *Vaughan,* 65 C.A.2d Supp. 844, 150 P.2d 964 (1944); *Watchtower Bible and Tract Society* v. *Metropolitan Life Insurance Co.,* 297 N.Y. 339, 79 N.E.2d 433 (1948), *cert. denied,* 335 U.S. 886 (1948). A total prohibition of door-bell ringing by Jehovah's Witnesses was held unconstitutional by a 5 to 4 vote in *Martin* v. *City of Struthers,* 319 U.S. 141 (1943).

65 See *State* ex rel. *Wisconsin Lutheran High School Conf.* v. *Sinar,* 267 Wis. 91, 65 N.W.2d 43 (1954); *Corp. of Presiding Bishop* v. *City of Porterville,* 90 Cal. App. 2d 656, 203 P.2d 823 (1949), *appeal dismissed for want of a substantial federal question,* 338 U.S. 805 (1949). Consult: Paul Brindel, "Zoning Out Religious Institutions," *Notre Dame Lawyer,* XXXII (August, 1957), 627–641; Note: "Churches and Zoning," *Harvard Law Review,* LXX (June, 1957), 1428–1438.

66 See, e.g., *Dalton* v. *St. Luke's Catholic Church,* 27 N.J. 22, 141 A.2d 273 (1958).

67 See, e.g., *Glaser* v. *Congregation Kehillath Israel,* 263 Mass. 435, 161 N.E. 619 (1928).

68 *In re Summers,* 325 U.S. 561 (1945).

69 *Baxley* v. *United States,* 134 F.2d 937 (4th Cir. 1943); *Gara* v. *United States,* 178 F.2d 38 (6th Cir. 1949), *affirmed by an equally divided Court,* 340 U.S. 857 (1950).

70 *Hamilton* v. *Regents,* 293 U.S. 245 (1934).

71 *Rice* v. *Commonwealth,* 188 Va. 224, 49 S.E.2d 342, 3 A.L.R.2d 1392 (1948); *Commonwealth* v. *Beiler,* 168 Pa. Super. 462, 79 A.2d 134 (1952); *Commonwealth* v. *Bey,* 166 Pa. Super. 136, 70 A.2d 693 (1950).

72 *Cox* v. *New Hampshire,* 312 U.S. 569 (1941).

73 *Theory of Legislation* (London, Trübner & Co., 1876), p. 86.

74 *Dennis* v. *United States,* 341 U.S. 494, 508 (1951).

75 See: W. G. Torpey, *Judicial Doctrines of Religious Rights in America* (Chapel Hill: University of North Carolina Press, 1948), Chap. 6; Claude W. Stimson, "The Exemption of Churches from Taxation," *Taxes,* XVIII (June, 1940), 361–364, 397; M. G. Paulsen, "Preferment of Religious Institutions in Tax and Labor Legislation," *Law and Contemporary Problems,* XIV (Winter, 1949), 144–159.

76 *M. E. Church, South* v. *Hinton,* 92 Tenn. 188, 21 S.W. 321, 322 (1893). Cf. the remarks of Gustave Weigel in John Cogley, ed., *Religion in America* (New York: Meridian Books, Inc., 1958), p. 231: "The more valid the religion the richer will be its manifestation of the virtues of unselfishness, sobriety, fulfillment of duty. These things are not just religious virtues but also positive contributions to the natural commonwealth, for the commonwealth cannot survive without them. It is precisely in this area that the civic community expects help from religion. The fruits of high religion are the love of man which results in help of the neighbor, self-control, industriousness, solidarity, patience and steadfastness. These fruits the political society wants. It does not care what they spring from."

77 *Garrett Biblical Institute* v. *Elmhurst State Bank,* 331 Ill. 308, 163 N.E. 1 (1928).

78 See 62 Stat. 613 (1948), *as amended,* 50 U.S.C. App. §456(j) (1952); 66 Stat. 258 (1952), 8 U.S.C. §1448 (1952); *Berman* v. *United States,* 156 F.2d 377 (9th Cir. 1946), *cert. denied,* 329 U.S. 795 (1946); *George* v. *United States,* 196 F.2d 445 (9th Cir. 1952), *cert. denied,* 344 U.S. 843 (1952). Consult: M. P. Sibley and Philip E. Jacob, *Conscription of Conscience* (Ithaca: Cornell University Press, 1952).

79 *Davis* v. *Beason,* 133 U.S. 333, 342 (1890).

80 *United States* v. *Macintosh,* 283 U.S. 605, 633 (1931) (dissenting opinion). The Chief Judge of the federal District Court for the Southern District of California, Leon R. Yankwich, recently reviewed the authorities and concluded that "the standard or accepted understanding of the meaning of 'Religion' in American society" is "the relationship of the individual to a Supreme Being." *George* v. *United States,* 196 F.2d 445 (9th Cir. 1952), *cert. denied,* 344 U.S. 843 (1952). For similar views, see *Cline* v. *State,* 9 Okla. Cr. 40, 130 P. 510 (1913); *Berman* v. *United States,* 156 F.2d 377 (9th Cir. 1946), *cert. denied,* 329 U.S. 795 (1946); *Opinion of the Justices,* 309 Mass. 555, 34 N.E.2d 431 (1941).

81 *The Varieties of Religious Experience* (New York: Longmans, Green, 1923), p. 31.

82 *Washington Ethical Society* v. *District of Columbia,* 249 F.2d 127 (D.C. Cir. 1957).

83 *Fellowship of Humanity* v. *County of Alameda,* 153 C.A.2d 673, 315 P.2d 394 (Cal. App. 1st Dist., 1957).

84 *Terrett* v. *Taylor,* 9 Cranch (U.S.) 43 (1815).

85 *Bradfield* v. *Roberts,* 175 U.S. 291 (1899). In *Reuben Quick Bear* v. *Leupp,* 210 U.S. 50 (1908), the Court ruled that Indian tribal and trust funds may be used to pay for the education of Indians in sectarian schools.

86 Selective Draft Law Cases, 245 U.S. 366 (1918).

87 J. Field, in *Soon Hing* v. *Crowley,* 113 U.S. 703, 710 (1885). See A. W. Johnson and Frank H. Yost, *Separation of Church and State in the United States* (Minneapolis: University of Minnesota Press, 1948), Chaps. 19–20.

88 See the invaluable Research Bulletin of the National Education Association, *The State and Sectarian Education,* XXXIV, No. 4 (December, 1956). See also E. A. Walter, ed., *Religion and the State University* (Ann Arbor: University of Michigan Press, 1958); R. F. Butts, *The American Tradition in Religion and Education* (Boston: Beacon Press, 1950).

89 *People* ex rel. *Ring* v. *Board of Education,* 245 Ill. 334, 349, 92 N.E. 251, 256, 29 L.R.A. (N.S.) 442, 19 Ann. Cas. 220 (1910).

90 The authorities are collected in Robert F. Cushman, "The Holy Bible and the Public Schools," *Cornell Law Quarterly,* XL (Spring, 1955), 475–499.

91 *Illinois* ex rel. *McCollum* v. *Board of Education,* 333 U.S. 203 (1948). For an analysis of the dissenting view, see F. W. O'Brien, *Justice Reed and the First Amendment* (Georgetown University Press), Chaps. 8–9.

92 *Zorach* v. *Clausen,* 343 U.S. 306 (1952).

93 343 U.S. at 312.

94 *West Virginia State Board of Education* v. *Barnette,* 319 U.S. 624 (1943), *overruling Minersville School District* v. *Gobitis,* 310 U.S. 586 (1940).

95 See the cases cited in Note 71.

96 *Pierce* v. *Society of Sisters,* 268 U.S. 510 (1925).

97 *Meyer* v. *Nebraska,* 262 U.S. 390 (1923).

98 See Note, "Catholic Schools and Public Money," *Yale Law Journal,*

L (March, 1941), 917–927. The policy of Congress for the District of Columbia is set out in the following statutory language: "It is hereby declared to be the policy of the Government of the United States to make no appropriation of money or property for the purpose of founding, maintaining, or aiding by payment for services, expenses, or otherwise, any church or religious denomination, or any institution or society which is under sectarian or ecclesiastical control; and no money appropriated for charitable purposes in the District of Columbia, shall be paid to any church or religious denomination, or to any institution or society which is under sectarian or ecclesiastical control." 29 Stat. 411 (1896), D.C. CODE §32–1008 (1951).

99 *Donoghue* v. *Smith*, 119 Vt. 259, 126 A.2d 93 (1956); *Almond* v. *Day*, 197 Va. 419, 89 S.E.2d 851 (1955). See also: *In re Opinion of the Justices*, 214 Mass. 599, 102 N.E. 464 (1913); *Otken* v. *Lamkin*, 56 Miss. 758 (1879); *Underwood* v. *Wood*, 93 Ky. 177, 19 S.W. 405 (1892); *Atchison, T., and S.F.R.R.* v. *City of Atchison*, 47 Kan. 712, 28 Pac. 1000 (1892); *Synod of Dakota* v. *State*, 2 S.D. 366, 50 N.W. 632, 14 L.R.A. 418 (1891).

100 *Cochran* v. *Louisiana State Board of Education*, 281 U.S. 370 (1930).

101 *Adams* v. *Commissioners*, 180 Md. 550, 26 A.2d 377 (1942); *Board of Education* v. *Wheat*, 174 Md. 314, 199 Atl. 628 (1938); *State* ex rel. *Van Straten* v. *Milquet*, 180 Wis. 109, 192 N.W. 392 (1923); *Costigan* v. *Hall*, 249 Wis. 94, 23 N.W.2d 495 (1946).

102 *Everson* v. *Board of Education*, 330 U.S. 1 (1947).

103 The citations are collected in David Fellman, "Separation of Church and State in the United States: A Summary View," *Wisconsin Law Review*, 1950 (May, 1950), 427–478, at 473–475.

104 For a recent holding to this effect, see *Hackett* v. *Hackett*, 150 N.E.2d 431 (Ohio Ct. App. 1958), noted in *Harvard Law Review*, LXXII (December, 1958), 372–374. See also: Leo Pfeffer, "Religion in the Upbringing of Children," *Boston University Law Review*, XXXV (June, 1955), 333–393; Leo M. Friedman, "The Parental Right to Control the Religious Education of a Child," *Harvard Law Review*, XXIX (March, 1916), 485–500; Note: "Enforceability of Antenuptial Contracts in Mixed Marriages," *Yale Law Journal*, L (May, 1941), 1286–1294; Note: "Religion as a Factor in Adoption, Guardianship and Custody," *Columbia Law Review*, LIV (March, 1954), 376–395.

105 "Religion and Education," *Religious Education*, XLVIII (November-December, 1953), 371–373, at 373.

The Right to Communicate

1   Morris L. Ernst, *The First Freedom* (New York: Macmillan, 1946).

2   *United States* v. *Carolene Products Co.,* 304 U.S. 144, 152, n.4 (1938). See Alpheus T. Mason, "The Core of Free Government, 1938–40: Mr. Justice Stone and 'Preferred Freedoms,'" *Yale Law Journal,* LXV (April, 1956), 597–628; Samuel J. Konefsky, *Chief Justice Stone and the Supreme Court* (New York: Macmillan, 1945), pp. 269–275.

3   See *Thomas* v. *Collins,* 323 U.S. 516, 530 (1945): ". . . the usual presumption supporting legislation is balanced by the preferred place given in our scheme to the great, the indispensable democratic freedoms secured by the First Amendment. . . . That priority gives these liberties a sanctity and a sanction not permitting dubious intrusions." See also the remarks of Justice Roberts in *Schneider* v. *Irvington,* 308 U.S. 147, 161 (1939).

4   See Burton C. Bernard, "Avoidance of Constitutional Issues in the United States Supreme Court: Liberties of the First Amendment," *Michigan Law Review,* L (December, 1951), 261–296, 267, 269.

5   *West Virginia State Board of Education* v. *Barnette,* 319 U.S. 624, 648 (1943) (dissenting opinion).

6   *Kovacs* v. *Cooper,* 336 U.S. 77, 90 (1949) (concurring opinion). For a detailed argument on this point, see Henry Steele Commager, *Majority Rule and Minority Rights* (New York: Oxford, 1943).

7   *Dennis* v. *United States,* 341 U.S. 494, 526 (1951).

8   *Sweezy* v. *New Hampshire,* 354 U.S. 234, 265–266 (1957).

9   *Kovacs* v. *Cooper,* 336 U.S. 77, 95 (1949) (concurring opinion).

10   See Edmond Cahn, "The Firstness of the First Amendment," *Yale Law Journal,* LXV (February, 1956), 464–481.

11   *Downes* v. *Bidwell,* 182 U.S. 244 (1901); *Hawaii* v. *Mankichi,* 190 U.S. 197 (1903); *Dorr* v. *United States,* 195 U.S. 138 (1904); *Balzac* v. *Porto Rico,* 258 U.S. 298 (1922). For a review of the same general problem in the period following World War II, see Charles Fairman, "Some New Problems of the Constitution Following the Flag," *Stanford Law Review,* I (June, 1949), 587–645.

12 *Adamson* v. *California,* 332 U.S. 46 (1947).

13 *Gitlow* v. *New York,* 268 U.S. 652 (1925). See Charles Warren, "The New 'Liberty' under the Fourteenth Amendment," *Harvard Law Review,* XXXIX (February, 1926), 431–465.

14 *Near* v. *Minnesota,* 283 U.S. 697 (1931).

15 *Powell* v. *Alabama,* 287 U.S. 45 (1932).

16 *Hurtado* v. *California,* 110 U.S. 516 (1884).

17 *Twining* v. *New Jersey,* 211 U.S. 78 (1908).

18 For a convenient short collection of opinions from such sources as these, see Howard Mumford Jones, ed., *Primer of Intellectual Freedom* (Cambridge: Harvard University Press, 1949).

19 *The Faith of a Liberal* (New York: Holt, 1946).

20 *Freedom, Loyalty, Dissent* (New York: Oxford, 1954). See also John W. Caughey, *In Clear and Present Danger* (Chicago: University of Chicago Press, 1958).

21 *Free Speech in the United States* (Cambridge: Harvard University Press, 1948).

22 See Elmer H. Davis, *But We Were Born Free* (Indianapolis: Bobbs, Merrill, 1954); Alan Barth, *The Loyalty of Free Men* (New York: Viking, 1951).

23 *Dennis* v. *United States,* 341 U.S. 494, 550 (1951).

24 *Id.,* at 503.

25 *Id.,* at 580.

26 *Id.,* at 584.

27 *Abrams* v. *United States,* 250 U.S. 616, 630 (1919) (dissenting opinion).

28 *Areopagitica* (Everyman's Library ed.), p. 24.

29 See Merle Curti, "Human Nature in American Thought," *Political Science Quarterly,* LXVIII (September, 1953), 354–375; (December, 1953), 492–510.

30 *Dennis* v. *United States,* 341 U.S. 494, 584 (1951) (dissenting opinion).

31 *Whitney* v. *California,* 274 U.S. 357, 377 (1927) (concurring opinion).

32 *De Jonge* v. *Oregon,* 299 U.S. 353, 365 (1937).

33 *West Virginia State Board of Education* v. *Barnette,* 319 U.S. 624, 636 (1943).

34 See, e.g., their dissenting opinions in *Dennis* v. *United States,* 341 U.S. 494, 579, 581 (1951), and their concurring opinion in *Yates* v. *United States,* 354 U.S. 298, 339 (1957).

35 *Free Speech and Its Relation to Self-Government* (New York: Harper, 1948), p. 17.

36 *Id.*, pp. 18–19.

37 Walter Berns, *Freedom, Virtue and the First Amendment* (Baton Rouge; Louisiana State University Press, 1957), p. 46.

38 See Robert K. Murray, *Red Scare* (Minneapolis: University of Minnesota Press, 1955).

39 *Frohwerk v. United States,* 249 U.S. 204, 206 (1919).

40 *Free Speech in the United States,* p. 3.

41 Ala. Const., Art. I, §4. For similar declarations, see Alaska Const., Art. I, §5; Ariz. Const., Art. II, §6; Ark. Const., Art. I, §6; Calif. Const., Art. I, §9; Conn. Const., Art. I, §5; Colo. Const., Art. II, §10; Del. Const., Art. I, §5; Fla. Const., Decl. of Rights, §13; Ga. Const., Art. I, §2–115; Ida. Const., Art. I, §9; Ill. Const., Art. II, §4; Ind. Const., Art. I, §9; Iowa Const., Art. I, §7; Kans. Const., Bill of Rights, §11; Ky. Const., Bill of Rights, §8; La. Const., Bill of Rights, Art. 3; Me. Const., Art. 1, §4; Md. Const., Decl. of Rights, §40; Mich. Const., Art. II, §4; Minn. Const., Art. I, §3; Mo. Const., Art. I, §8; Mont. Const., Art. III, §10; Nebr. Const., Art. I, §5; Nev. Const., Art. I, §9; N.J. Const., Art. 1, §6; N.M. Const., Art. II, §17; N.Y. Const., Art. 1, §8; N.C. Const., Art. I, §20; N.D. Const., Art. I, §9; Ohio Const., Art. I, §11; Okla. Const., Art. II, §22; Ore. Const., Art. I, §8; Pa. Const., Art. I, §7; R.I. Const., Art. I, §20; S.D. Const., Art. VI, §5; Tenn. Const., Art. I, §19; Tex. Const., Art. I, §8; Va. Const., Art. I, §12; Wash. Const., Art. I, §5; Wisc. Const., Art. I, §3; Wyo. Const., Art. I, §20.

42 W. Va. Const., Art. III, §7.

43 See Jeremiah Smith, "Liability for Negligent Language," *Harvard Law Review,* XIV (November, 1900), 184–199.

44 For an excellent review, see "Developments in the Law: Defamation," *Harvard Law Review,* LXIX (March, 1956), 875–960.

45 *Restatement of Torts,* Vol. 3, §559 (1938). See Philip Wittenberg, *Dangerous Words* (New York: Columbia University Press, 1947).

46 See Ark. Const., Art. II, §6; Calif. Const., Art. I, §9; Fla. Const., Decl. of Rights, §13; Ill. Const., Art. II, §4; Iowa Const., Art. I, §7; Kans. Const., Bill of Rights, §11; Mich. Const., Art. II, §18; Miss. Const., Art. III, §13; Nebr. Const., Art. I, §5; Nev. Const., Art. I, §9; N.J. Const., Art. I, §6; N.M. Const., Art. II, §17; N.Y. Const., Art. I, §8; N.D. Const., Art. I, §9; Ohio Const., Art. I, §11; Okla. Const., Art. II, §22; R.I. Const.,

Art. I, §20; Tex. Const., Art. I, §8; Utah Const., Art. I, §15; W.Va. Const., Art. III, §8; Wisc. Const., Art. I, §3.

47 *Foltz* v. *Moore McCormack Lines,* 189 F.2d 537 (2nd. Cir. 1951).

48 *Carr* v. *Hood,* 1 Campbell's Reports, 355, 358, 170 Eng. Rep. 983, 985 (1808).

49 *Cartwright* v. *Herald Pub. Co.,* 220 S.C. 492, 68 S.E.2d 415 (1951).

50 *See Restatement of Torts,* §606(1).

51 *Mencher* v. *Chesley,* 297 N.Y. 94, 75 N.E.2d 257 (1947).

52 J. L. Globensky and L. G. Sculthorp, "Defamation—Libelous Per Se—Imputation that One Is a Communist," *Notre Dame Lawyer,* XXIV (Summer, 1949), 542–549, 542.

53 *Spanel* v. *Pegler,* 160 F.2d 619, 622, 171 A.L.R. 699 (7th Cir. 1947). See also *Utah State Farm Bureau Federation* v. *National Farmers Union Service Corporation,* 198 F.2d 20, 33 A.L.R.2d 1186 (10th Cir. 1952), which upheld an award of $25,000 against an organization which asserted that another organization was "Communist-dominated." The Court said: ". . . it is now the generally accepted view that to write or speak of a person or an organization as being 'communist' or a 'communist sympathizer' is to subject such person or organization to public hatred, odium and contempt, to his immediate harm, and is therefore libelous per se."

54 *Christopher* v. *American News Co.,* 171 F.2d 275 (7th Cir. 1948); *Derounian* v. *Stokes,* 168 F.2d 305 (10th Cir. 1948); *O'Donnell* v. *Philadelphia Record Co.,* 356 Pa. 307, 51 A.2d 775 (1947).

55 See Note, "Protection from Defamation in Congressional Hearings," *University of Chicago Law Review,* XVI (Spring, 1949), 544–554; Willard H. Pedrick, "Senator McCarthy and the Law of Libel: A Study of Two Campaign Speeches," *Northwestern University Law Review,* XLVIII (May-June, 1953), 135–184. For a recent decision on this point, see *Tenney* v. *Brandhove,* 341 U.S. 367 (1951).

56 For a debate on this question, see Nathan D. Perlman and Morris Ploscowe, "False Defamatory Anti-Racial and Anti-Religious Propaganda and the Use of the Mails," *Lawyers Guild Review,* IV (January-February, 1944), 13–23; O.K. Fraenkel, "The Lynch Bill—A Different View," *Lawyers Guild Review,* IV (March-April, 1944), 12–15.

57 See David Riesman, "Democracy and Defamation," *Columbia Law Review,* XLII (May, November, December, 1942), 727–780, 1085–1123, 1282–1318; Loren P. Beth, "Group Libel and Free Speech," *Minnesota*

Law Review, XXXIX (January, 1955), 167–184; Note: "Group Libel Laws: Abortive Efforts to Combat Hate Propaganda," *Yale Law Journal*, LXI (February, 1952), 252–264.

58   *State* v. *Klapprott*, 127 N.J.L. 395, 22 A.2d 877 (1941).

59   *People* v. *Beauharnais*, 408 Ill. 512, 97 N.E.2d 343 (1951).

60   *Beauharnais* v. *Illinois*, 343 U.S. 250 (1952).

61   *Id.*, at 259.

62   *Id.*, at 270.

63   *Id.*, at 286.

64   See, e.g., *People* v. *Spielman*, 318 Ill. 482, 149 N.E. 466 (1925) (American Legion); *People* v. *Turner*, 28 Cal. App. 766, 154 Pac. 34 (1915) (Knights of Columbus); *Jones* v. *State*, 38 Tex. Crim. 364, 43 S.W. 78 (1897) (city railway conductors of Irish descent); *State* v. *Hoskins*, 60 Minn. 168, 62 N.W. 270 (1895) (three banks).

65   See *People* v. *Edmondson*, 168 Misc. 142, 4 N.Y.S.2d 257 (N.Y. County Ct. 1938).

66   Ill. Rev. Stat. c. 38, §471 (1955).

67   Ind. Ann. Stat. §10–904 (Burns Supp. 1953).

68   Mass. Ann. Stat. c. 272, §98C (Supp. 1954).

69   Nev. Comp. Laws §10110 (1929).

70   Conn. Gen. Stat. §8376 (1949).

71   W.Va. Code Ann. §6109 (1955).

72   N.M. Stat. Ann. §40–27–25–7 (1953).

73   For illustrations, see Joseph Tanenhaus, "Group Libel: Who Controls the United States," *Cornell Law Quarterly*, XXXV (Winter, 1950), 261–302, at 283–285.

74   Zechariah Chafee, Jr., *Government and Mass Communications* (Chicago: University of Chicago Press, 1947), I, 125.

75   *Id.*, I, 128.

76   See Tanenhaus, at 288.

77   337 U.S. 1 (1949). See Note, *"Freedom of Speech v. Breach of the Peace,"* *St. John's Law Review*, XXV (1951), 295–305.

78   *Id.*, at 4.

79   *Id.*, at 14.

80   *Id.*, at 36–37.

81   *Chaplinsky* v. *New Hampshire*, 315 U.S. 568 (1942). See John W. Wade, "Tort Liability for Abusive and Insulting Language," *Vanderbilt Law Review*, IV (December, 1950), 63–115.

82 *Valentine* v. *Chrestensen*, 316 U.S. 52 (1942).

83 *Feiner* v. *New York*, 340 U.S. 315 (1951). See L. Saulson, "Municipal Control of Public Streets and Parks as Affecting Freedom of Speech and Assembly," *Michigan Law Review*, XLXIX (June, 1951), 1185–1199; Note: "Free Speech and the Hostile Audience," *New York University Law Review*, XXVI (July, 1951), 489–505.

84 *Poulos* v. *New Hampshire*, 345 U.S. 395 (1953); *Cox* v. *New Hampshire*, 312 U.S. 569 (1941).

85 *Niemotko* v. *Maryland*, 340 U.S. 268 (1951); *Kunz* v. *New York*, 340 U.S. 290 (1951).

86 *Niemotko* v. *Maryland*, 340 U.S. at 271, 272.

87 *Schneider* v. *State*, 308 U.S. 147 (1939). An ordinance forbidding the distribution of anonymous handbills was upheld in *People* v. *Arnold*, 127 Cal. App.2d 844, 273 P.2d 711 (1954), noted in *University of Pennsylvania Law Review*, CIII (December, 1954), 437–440.

88 *Milwaukee County* v. *Carter*, 258 Wis. 139, 45 N.W.2d 90 (1950).

89 *Martin* v. *City of Struthers*, 319 U.S. 141 (1943).

90 *Bread* v. *Alexandria*, 341 U.S. 622 (1951).

91 *Saia* v. *New York*, 334 U.S. 558 (1948).

92 *Kovacs* v. *Cooper*, 336 U.S. 77 (1949).

93 See *Brinkman* v. *City of Gainesville*, 83 Ga. 508, 64 S.E.2d 344 (1951), and the state authorities cited therein.

94 *Thornhill* v. *Alabama*, 310 U.S. 88 (1940).

95 *Carlson* v. *California*, 310 U.S. 106, 112–113 (1940).

96 *A.F. of L.* v. *Swing*, 312 U.S. 321 (1941); *Cafeteria Employees Union* v. *Angelos*, 320 U.S. 293 (1943).

97 *Bakery & Pastry Drivers & Helpers Local* v. *Wohl*, 315 U.S. 769 (1942).

98 *International Brotherhood of Teamsters* v. *Vogt*, 354 U.S. 284, 296 (1957) (dissenting opinion). See Edgar A. Jones, "Picketing and the Communication of Ideas," *U.C.L.A. Law Review*, II (February, 1955), 212–223.

99 *Milk Wagon Drivers Union* v. *Meadowmoor Dairies*, 312 U.S. 287 (1941). For more recent decisions on this point, see *Cole* v. *Arkansas*, 338 U.S. 345 (1949). The Court held in *Allen-Bradley Local* v. *Wisconsin Employment Relations Board*, 315 U.S. 740 (1942), that the state's power to deal with picketing in a context of violence is not precluded by the National Labor Relations Act.

100 *Carpenters & Joiners Union* v. *Ritter's Cafe,* 315 U.S. 722 (1942).

101 *Giboney* v. *Empire Storage and Ice Co.,* 336 U.S. 490 (1949). In *Local Union No. 10, A.F. of L.* v. *Graham,* 345 U.S. 192 (1953), the Court held that Virginia may enjoin peaceful picketing when its purpose is in conflict with the state "right-to-work" statute which outlaws the closed shop as well as the "yellow-dog" contract. Of course, the same general rule holds where a federal statute defines the forbidden conduct: *International Brotherhood of Electrical Workers* v. *N.L.R.B.,* 341 U.S. 694 (1951).

102 *Building Service Employees International Union* v. *Gazzam,* 339 U.S. 532 (1950).

103 *Hughes* v. *Superior Court of California,* 339 U.S. 460 (1950); *International Brotherhood of Teamsters* v. *Hanke,* 339 U.S. 470 (1950).

104 *Hughes* v. *Superior Court of California,* 339 U.S. at 465–466.

105 The leading precedents were fully reviewed by Justice Frankfurter in *International Brotherhood of Teamsters* v. *Vogt,* 354 U.S. 284 (1957). See also *Youngdahl* v. *Rainfair,* 355 U.S. 131 (1957).

106 The federal interest began with the Tariff Act of 1842, 5 Stat. 548, 566, which forbade the importation of obscene literature. The mailing of such literature was first prohibited by the Comstock Act of 1872, 17 Stat. 282, 302. Since 1842, Congress has adopted some twenty obscenity laws.

107 *Roth* v. *United States,* 354 U.S. 476, 484 (1957). In the following paragraphs I have drawn freely from a pamphlet I once wrote on *The Censorship of Books* (Madison: University of Wisconsin Press, 1957).

108 *People* v. *Hildabridle,* 353 Mich. 562, 92 N.W.2d 6, 13 (1958).

109 *Id.,* 92 N.W.2d at 14.

110 *Id.,* 92 N.W.2d at 19.

111 *Id.*

112 *Regina* v. *Hicklin,* Law Reports, 3 Q.B. 360, 371 (1868).

113 *United States* v. *One Book Called "Ulysses,"* 5 F. Supp. 182 (S.D. N.Y. 1933), *affirmed,* 72 F.2d 705 (2nd Cir. 1934), by Judges Augustus N. and Learned Hand.

114 *Commonwealth* v. *Gordon,* 66 D.& C. (Penna.), 101, 125 (1949).

115 *Id.,* at 137–138.

116 *Government and Mass Communications,* I, 210–215. In *Bonica* v. *Olesen,* 126 F. Supp. 398 (S.D. Cal. 1954), Judge Ernest A. Tolin identified fourteen different definitions of obscenity.

117 See, e.g., the opinion of Judge Charles Andrews of the New York

Court of Appeals, in *People* v. *Muller,* 96 N.Y. 408, 410 (1884). Since Judge Andrews thought that "every person of ordinary intelligence" readily recognizes what is obscene, he ruled that the testimony of experts was both unnecessary and inappropriate.

118 See Anne Lyon Haight, *Banned Books* (2d ed., New York: R.R. Bowker Co., 1955); Morris L. Ernst and William Seagle, *To the Pure* (New York: Viking, 1928); Morris L. Ernst and Alexander Lindey, *The Censor Marches On* (New York: Doubleday, Doran, 1940).

119 352 U.S. 380.

120 354 U.S. 476.

121 *Id.* at 487.

122 *Id.* at 500.

123 *Id.* at 489.

124 *Id.* at 514.

125 In *Roth* v. *United States,* 354 U.S. 476 (1957), and *Kingsley Books* v. *Brown,* 354 U.S. 436 (1957). On the authority of these cases the Court upheld the banning of burlesque shows in Newark, in *Adams Newark Theater Co.* v. *City of Newark,* 354 U.S. 931 (1957).

126 *Mounce* v. *United States,* 355 U.S. 180 (1957); *One, Inc.* v. *Olesen,* 355 U.S. 371 (1958); *Sunshine Book Co.* v. *Summerfield,* 355 U.S. 372 (1958); *Time Film Corp.* v. *Chicago,* 355 U.S. 35 (1957). See Philip M. Carden, "The Supreme Court and Obscenity," *Vanderbilt Law Review,* XI (March, 1958), 585–598.

The Right to Talk Politics

1 *The Nature and Destiny of Man,* Vol. II: *Human Destiny* (New York: Scribner, 1941), p. 268.

2 John Milton, *Areopagitica* (Everyman's ed.), p. 32.

3 See Erich Fromm, *Escape from Freedom* (New York: Farrar & Rinehart, 1941).

4 *Whitney* v. *California,* 274 U.S. 357, 377 (1927) (concurring opinion).

5 *Id.* at 375.

6 *Wieman* v. *Updegraff,* 344 U.S. 183, 193 (1952) (concurring opinion).

7 *Yates* v. *United States,* 354 U.S. 298, 344 (1957) (separate opinion).

8 *United States* v. *Schwimmer,* 279 U.S. 644, 654 (1929) (dissenting opinion).

9 *American Communications Association* v. *Douds,* 339 U.S. 382, 442–443 (1950) (separate opinion).

10 *Near* v. *Minnesota,* 283 U.S. 697, 722 (1931).

11 *Dennis* v. *United States,* 341 U.S. 494, 502 (1951).

12 *Id.* at 550.

13 *International Brotherhood of Electrical Workers* v. *National Labor Relations Board,* 181 F.2d 34, 40 (2nd Cir. 1950).

14 See Livingston Rutherford, *John Peter Zenger* (New York: Dodd, Mead, 1904).

15 *Free Speech in the United States* (Cambridge: Harvard University Press, 1948), p. 21.

16 See James M. Smith, *Freedom's Fetters* (Ithaca: Cornell University Press, 1956); John C. Miller, *Crisis in Freedom* (Boston: Little, Brown, 1951).

17 Act of July 14, 1798, 1 Stat. 596.

18 See Clement Eaton, *Freedom of Thought in the Old South* (Durham, N.C.: Duke University Press, 1940); Russel B. Nye, *Fettered Freedom* (East Lansing: Michigan State College Press, 1949); James E. Cutler, *Lynch Law* (New York: Longmans, Green, 1905), Chap. 4.

19 See James G. Randall, *Constitutional Problems under Lincoln* (rev. ed., Urbana: University of Illinois Press, 1951), Chaps. 6–8.

20 Act of June 15, 1917, 40 Stat. 217; Act of May 16, 1918, 40 Stat. 553.

21 Louis F. Post, *The Deportations Delirium of Nineteen-Twenty* (Chicago: C. H. Kerr, 1923). See Robert W. Dunn, ed., *The Palmer Raids* (New York: International Publishers, 1948); Robert K. Murray, *Red Scare: A Study in National Hysteria, 1919–1920* (Minneapolis: University of Minnesota Press, 1955).

22 For Hughes' great speech on this occasion, see *Report of the New York State Bar Association,* XLIII (1920), 533–545. See also Merlo J. Pusey, *Charles Evans Hughes* (New York: Macmillan, 1951), I, 391–393.

23 See Chafee, *Free Speech in the United States,* pp. 247–269.

24 See G. Louis Joughin and Edmund M. Morgan, *The Legacy of Sacco and Vanzetti* (New York: Harcourt, Brace, 1948).

25 See Zechariah Chafee, Jr., *Thirty-Five Years with Freedom of Speech* (New York, 1952).

26 *United Public Workers* v. *Mitchell,* 330 U.S. 75 (1947).

27 Act of July 19, 1940, 54 Stat. 767, c. 640, 18 U.S.C.A. §61a.

28 *Bailey* v. *Richardson,* 182 F.2d 46 (App. D.C. 1950).

29 *Id.* at 59.

30 341 U.S. 918 (1951).

31 See *Peters* v. *Hobby,* 349 U.S. 331 (1955); *Cole* v. *Young,* 351 U.S. 536 (1956); *Service* v. *Dulles,* 354 U.S. 363 (1957). See Ralph S. Brown, *Loyalty and Security* (New Haven: Yale University Press, 1958); Eleanor Bontecou, *The Federal Loyalty-Security Program* (Ithaca: Cornell University Press, 1953); David Fellman, *The Defendant's Rights* (New York: Rinehart, 1958), Chap. 12.

32 *Garner* v. *Board of Public Works of Los Angeles,* 341 U.S. 716 (1951).

33 *Adler* v. *Board of Education of City of New York,* 342 U.S. 485 (1952).

34 *Id.* at 492.

35 *Id.* at 496–497.

36 *American Communications Association* v. *Douds,* 339 U.S. 382 (1950). See Comment, *Yale Law Journal,* LVII (March, 1948), 806–827.

37 Act of June 23, 1947, 61 Stat. 136, 146, 29 U.S.C.A. §§141, 159(h).

38 See *Cramer* v. *United States,* 325 U.S. 1 (1945). For a conviction that did stand up on appeal, see *Haupt* v. *United States,* 330 U.S. 631 (1947).

39 *Hartzel* v. *United States,* 322 U.S. 680 (1944).

40 *Near* v. *Minnesota,* 283 U.S. 697 (1931).

41 *De Jonge* v. *Oregon,* 299 U.S. 353 (1937); *Herndon* v. *Lowry,* 301 U.S. 242 (1937).

42 *De Jonge* v. *Oregon,* 299 U.S. at 365.

43 *Fiske* v. *Kansas,* 274 U.S. 380 (1927).

44 *Stromberg* v. *California,* 283 U.S. 359 (1931).

45 *Herndon* v. *Lowry,* 301 U.S. 242, 258 (1937).

46 *Schneiderman* v. *United States,* 320 U.S. 118 (1943).

47 *Thomas* v. *Collins,* 323 U.S. 516 (1945).

48 *United States* v. *C.I.O.,* 335 U.S. 106 (1948).

49 *Id.* at 143.

50 *Dennis* v. *United States,* 341 U.S. 494 (1951).

51 See Wallace Mendelson, "Clear and Present Danger—from Schenck to Dennis," *Columbia Law Review,* LII (March, 1952), 313–333.

52 *Schenck* v. *United States,* 249 U.S. 47 (1919).

53 *Whitney* v. *California,* 274 U.S. 357, 377 (1947) (concurring opinion).

54 *Schenck* v. *United States,* 249 U.S. 47 (1919); *Frohwerk* v. *United States,* 249 U.S. 204 (1919); *Debs* v. *United States,* 249 U.S. 211 (1919).

55 *Abrams* v. *United States,* 250 U.S. 616 (1919); *Schaefer* v. *United States,* 251 U.S. 466 (1920); *Pierce* v. *United States,* 252 U.S. 239 (1920).

56 See Robert E. Cushman, " 'Clear and Present Danger' in Free Speech Cases: A Study in Judicial Semantics," in Milton R. Konvitz and Arthur E. Murphy, eds., *Essays in Political Theory* (Ithaca: Cornell University Press, 1948), pp. 311–324.

57 *Gitlow* v. *New York,* 268 U.S. 652 (1925).

58 *Free Speech in the United States,* p. 319.

59 *Dennis* v. *United States,* 341 U.S. 494 (1951).

60 *United States* v. *Foster,* 9 F.R.D. 367, 391 (1949).

61 *United States* v. *Dennis,* 183 F.2d 201 (2nd Cir. 1950).

62 *Id.,* at 216.

63 See his opinions in *De Jonge* v. *Oregon,* 299 U.S. 353 (1937), and in *Near* v. *Minnesota,* 283 U.S. 697 (1931).

64 See his dissenting opinion in *Minersville School District* v. *Gobitis,* 310 U.S. 586, 601 (1940).

65 *Pennekamp* v. *Florida,* 328 U.S. 331, 353 (1946) (concurring opinion).

66 *West Virginia State Board of Education* v. *Barnette,* 319 U.S. 624, 663 (1943) (dissenting opinion).

67 *Dennis* v. *United States,* 341 U.S. 494, 567 (1951) (concurring opinion).

68 *Id.,* at 568.

69 *Free Speech and Its Relation to Self-Government,* (New York: Harper, 1948), Chap. 2.

70 For a good collection of criticisms of the clear and present danger doctrine, see C. J. Antieau, " 'Clear and Present Danger'—Its Meaning and Significance," *Notre Dame Lawyer,* XXV (Summer, 1950), 603–645, 629–637.

71 Mendelson, *supra,* note 51, at p. 331.

72 *Standard Oil Co.* v. *United States,* 221 U.S. 1 (1911); *United States* v. *American Tobacco Co.,* 221 U.S. 106 (1911).

73 See Laurence Stapleton, *Justice and World Society* (Chapel Hill: University of North Carolina Press, 1944).

74 Paul A. Freund, *On Understanding the Supreme Court* (Boston: Little, Brown, 1950), pp. 27–28.

75 *United States* v. *Dennis,* 183 F.2d 201, 212 (2nd Cir. 1950).

76 *Dennis* v. *United States,* 341 U.S. 494, 519 (1951).

77 *Masses Pub. Co.* v. *Patten,* 244 Fed. 535, 540 (S.D. N.Y. 1917).

78 *Yates* v. *United States,* 354 U.S. 298, 318 (1957).

79 *Gitlow* v. *New York,* 268 U.S. 652, 664–665 (1925).

80 *United States* v. *Foster,* 9 F.R.D. 367, 391 (1949).

81 *Dennis* v. *United States,* 341 U.S. 494, 502 (1951).

82 *Id.,* at 545.

83 *Id.,* at 546.

84 *Id.,* at 572.

85 *Yates* v. *United States,* 354 U.S. 298 (1957).

86 *Id.,* at 324–325.